EVERY FAMILY'S HANDY GUIDE TO PREDICTION DURING SOCIAL DECLINE AND COLLAPSE

First Edition

DeVita

CONTENTS

INTRODUCTION

A Family's Handy Guide

What This Book Will Do: Help With Uncertainty.

When times are hard, uncertainty makes them worse. The changing weather is already hurting the food supply, and famine is a horrifying specter for all people. Hunger brings violence, and a decline in the value of people; everyone becomes a potential victim.

The social system, by which we mean all the people who grow our food, deliver it to our neighborhood, make sure the toilets flush and the water flows, keep us mostly safe in our homes, that system, is in trouble, and food shortages and transportation problems will make things worse.

Through all that change, we might like a little forewarning, a little glimpse of what might be next, and a way of discussing what the change might mean to our family. Uncertainty would still be there, but we would understand it more, and our guesses about what might come next would be more accurate than simply having no idea at all.

What This Book Won't Do: Tell You What To Do.

This book won't tell you what to store, where to live, or who to associate with. It intends to help you make those decisions yourself.

Family

This guide is to help families and groups determine, as much in advance and to the degree possible, what will happen in societal decline and collapse.

A family is a group of people, who may be related in different ways, but who share fate. They have common conceptions, and values, and goals. The have a value for the family itself.

If our family is large, that has an advantage in that we have many people to draw on for resources. It also means there will be a greater likelihood of subgroups forming, and that might have to be accommodated. If our family is small, we are more vulnerable in some ways, and have fewer hands to contribute, but likely, we will be more cohesive, and any surplus or profit shared more equally.

Each person in the family will have their own special talents.

Your family can be egalitarian, or hierarchical, or whatever you choose, whatever is most efficient and gives your family the most resilience. Your family lives in the system, and is part of it.

A logical way of approaching problems

Prediction is better than tea leaves, chicken livers, flocks of birds or psychoactive drug visions, tools people have used to predict the future.

We will talk about prediction and collapse. To accomplish that, many other concepts will necessarily be included, but those two are key, because our goal is to help navigate changing social circumstances through an informed strategy.

"Predict" means to tell something in advance (literally, "before-speak", or to say before it happens). Often, prediction is not difficult: a bus schedule is really a list of predictions about when the bus will arrive. Tide charts predict the rise and fall of tides. We predict what time family members should return home, to plan dinner.

Things that happen reliably, over and over, are somewhat easier to predict. But what about when things happen without that reliable pattern? We can understand that the ability to guess when the bus would come would be important when the buses ran infrequently and irregularly.

That brings us to "societal decline and collapse."

We use "societal collapse" to talk about a society which has stopped working. Collapse has been discussed in different ways, with slightly different definitions, which we can explore later, but for us, our family and friends, we mean things have stopped working.

Collapse can happen slowly, especially at first, and this is called "decline." It means things stop working as well as they did, but it is still possible to struggle on.

Collapse can happen very quickly. Suddenly, it seems nothing works.

We can also say it this way: collapse causes us to expect things to go wrong.

Being able to predict, when things have become unreliable, can save your people, or at least, increase the odds in that direction.

This small book is a guide: We expect to gain skills in understanding what is happening, and to improve our guesses about what will come next, but no one can tell you, in advance, what to do.

Once you have a group of predictions, what will you do? Whatever seems indicated by the situation: buy, sell, hunker down, step forward, pay for protection, fight, or flee.

Here is good advice for those who hope to survive, perhaps well:

Calm is a superpower.

--ATTRIBUTED TO BRUCE LEE

1. TWO KINDS OF SYSTEMS: THE PROBLEM OF THE BUS SCHEDULE

Complex And Linear Systems Are Different

There are scientific and philosophical discussions about what is "determined" and what is not. We can distill them all down to say that, whatever will happen is what is determined to happen. Sadly, even if it is determined, it is at such a level that it means nothing to us, we would need far too much information, we can't predict it, however determined it might be.

Well, what does that mean for us? What good is it to know that? It brings forward two important things for us to understand.

First, is that there are two basic types of systems, or things we want to predict.

One is linear, meaning things happen in a line, one after the other in a determined way. Consider a steam engine or internal combustion engine vehicle: The piston moves, the crankshaft turns, the valves open on intake and close on the pressure stage, the crankshaft turns the gear box, the wheels are propelled, the vehicle moves forward. That is a linear system. It can easily be predicted. A linear system can be *complicated* in its design, but it can still be predicted. In real life, few things are really linear.

Mostly, the systems we care about are *complex*, meaning different variables, that is, different parts, interact in a way that is not just one thing after another. It would be as if the piston were only connected to the crankshaft in some variable way. It would mean that the valves would only open and close under conditions which are difficult to identify.

We can talk about complex social systems as though they are discrete, meaning we initially discuss them as though they were separate, but in truth, they are subsystems, scattered across the globe, but still part of the one complex global social system.

We can talk about a city or a country as an individual system, but they are all linked in energy and resource pathways. By this, we mean trade and the movement of people. Almost no place on the planet is actually fully isolated at this point, and even those are dealing with climate change.

Even so, we can think and work on the things that matter most to us: our families, our communities, perhaps our nations, and talk about them as separate things. We just remember, we are placed in the greater complex system, what happens anywhere influences everywhere, but in ways we can't really predict.

Complex Systems Are Actually Energy Organized Through Networks

Consider a mountain stream or a lowlands river. It is just water flowing under the influence of gravity, interacting with the stream bed, usually rocks, gravel, sand and mud. Unless it is captive in a concrete ditch, the water has more movements to it than just flowing, down hill. If it did that, it would be a featureless ribbon of water. Instead, it is alive, with water roiling and patterns appearing and disappearing.

Let's place a large rock in the flow; the rock causes the flow to rise up into a wave or roil, and gravity pulls it back down, making the water bounce over the rock. However, the bounce is not regular, we can not predict exactly when it will come, or how high it will rise above the water.

Now we imagine many rocks of different sizes and locations. The flow of the water becomes nearly unpredictable. But, only nearly. We might not know when a pulse of water might occur, but we know it will. We can also watch it awhile and figure that most pulses occur within, say, 2 and 6 seconds, and none is longer than eight.

So, even though the complex system of the stream is just energy created from water and gravity, and though it is impossible to precisely predict its behavior, with careful watching and record keeping, we can make sense of the flow.

We would also realize another important feature of energy organized in complex systems: the stream also modifies the bed and bank. It is a feedback loop, with each influencing the other. The bed influences the stream of water immediately, and the stream influences the bed, on many scales from tiny eddies in stream bottom sand, to massive rocks, and it does so across scales of time, with some change on the small scale being almost ceaseless, and the movement of large rocks, infrequent, or very gradual.

We watch the water and the rocks, but what we see is energy, organizing itself.

Complex systems might be largely determined, but we have no way of getting and computing enough information to precisely predict. To us, they are unpredictable, though we can understand something about the behavior of those systems by watching their energy. In our case, what we want to know about is how energy is organizing around us; we are the medium.

The System Wraps Us Completely And Creates Context

Again, we remember that there is only one system and it is literally part of us, and we it. The system has been with us since we began to use tools, at least two million years ago, long before we were Homo sapiens sapiens (about 300,000 years ago). It is foundational to a thorough understanding to recognize that the system is a single complex system, organizing energy through human behavior and turning natural resources into humans.

Our first tool was likely a stick, then pebbles. As simple as those tools are, they had a significant effect on our ancestors. First of all, they made more food, that is energy, available, increasing the likelihood of our ancestors to live and reproduce (as we are evidence). However, it also changed behavior. To use a pebble, you must have a pebble, and so either find one nearby, or carry something: the unprocessed food to the pebble, or the pebble to the food. For the first time, perhaps, we had possessions, things we carried and became skilled at using.

Over time, a long time, our tools changed us. Our hand-eye coordination became more developed, and not just those portions of the brain, but also the social and cognitive portions. When the controlled use of fire became widespread, it allowed our ancestors to soften food, allowing less massive jaws and facial muscles, and sitting looking at each other around the fire encouraged vocal speech. The system made us more social.

The word "culture" refers to the features of that primary system. Nearly everything about us is culture: a computer, an internet, languages written, governments making laws and rules. What is often confused with "culture" is actually "custom," meaning the differences in the way culture is expressed, either by locale, or within a stratified social system. Culture is everything we have and do; custom is how we express it.

Having quickly described the very big picture, we can move on, because it might not be that pertinent to the immediacy of living daily life. Even so, knowing that the tools we use, and the procedures we follow, will shape our behavior; and knowing that virtually everything is connected to everything else in the human world, can help inform our predictions.

So, if we want good examples of complex systems, we can consider rivers and streams, the climate, the stock market and global society.

It Takes Energy To Organize A Complex System To Function As A Linear System

But, for a handy exercise, we will use the bus schedule as an example of both how intertwined the systems of our lives are, and how difficult it is to linearize a complex system. Millions of people use bus transportation; if your family does not, no matter.

You probably use some form of transportation, and predictability is still an issue, even if you walk[1]. Consider your daily schedule, and trips like shopping and doctor's appointments. In most cases, you are on some kind of schedule, and unreliable transportation makes your own scheduling difficult.

On its face, the bus schedule is linear. This bus comes here, then it goes here; another bus comes and it goes there, all on a predictable schedule, a nice network of moving buses. Under ideal conditions, predictions of bus behavior are pretty good. But not perfect, because the bus schedule is an attempt to make linear something that is complex.

So, it will work if everything goes right. But not if something changes, even some small, unforeseen thing. Something like a sports event, which would increase the use on one line, or, another example, if a bus route that served areas nearby didn't come, that would increase ridership as people sought the next most efficient route for their destination.

Let's, as an exercise, do a bus route.

We map out the service area, and determine what the big ridership draws are in each area. For example, a college, or a shopping center, or an airport, or geographic center of a subdivision. Those are our primary bus stops.

We will call those "nexuses and nodes", because they are places connected by many networks: roads, rivers, subway lines, airports, and seaports, for example. In our bus schedules, a library, museum, government building or school would be nexuses, connected by surface roads.

Then, we consider the streets that connect those places. We consider things like how many lanes a road has, and what the speed limit is, and how many vehicles use it at various times and days. The last is important to us, because our bus passenger rate will be related to traffic at those times, as many people move in different vehicles at the same time.

We could then consider the speed limits of the roads and streets of the route we designate, and estimate how long it takes a single passenger to get on or off, multiplied by the expected number of passengers, and we should be able to approximate how long it should take a bus to get from one stop to the next.

Do that for every stop on the route, and apply time to each: 14th and Donner at 12:45 and 14th and Plate by 12:58. Then, make that mesh with every other bus route so passengers can stop at one node and quickly take another bus to a node not on the first route. People need to be able to connect with different routes reliably.

And, here we note that, as the stream influenced the bed, the bus route influences the streets. The presence of a bus stop provides customers, some with minutes to wait, and so businesses from street stands to store fronts, accumulate there. If times are good, the business attracts more riders to that bus, for shops that have become destinations of their own.

But, things happen in the real world. Traffic effects the speed of the buses, making them late. Some stops have no riders, making the bus early. Sometimes a bus driver becomes ill, before work or while driving. Road construction can slow the bus. A bus might have mechanical problems.
Indeed, we can't even imagine all the real world situations which would increase or decrease the reliability of the bus to arrive on time. That is because the system, the energy of buses and people moving, are complex, and are changed by variables we can't imagine.

During normal times, when roads and streets are passable, and most people are law abiding and peaceful, and bus drivers can look forward to retirement, the energy flows smoothly. Since it is reliable, and relatively cheap as compared to driving and parking, or hiring a cab, people use it. The city grows around it, integrating the energy it carries into that of the city.

Indeed, we can see, as happens during "bus strikes," the system of the city suffers without the energy flow of the buses. The streets become clogged with private cars; people are late, and some just don't come to work, since it costs more to get there than they make.

None of that is on the bus schedule, we only know it because we watched the system closely and followed the energy. That is what we will do during decline and collapse.

2. ASHES, ASHES, WE ALL FALL DOWN

What Is Societal Collapse?

Oddly, this is not a simple thing to define in the moment to moment, experiential way we want to. This is because a functioning complex society rises and falls according to the amount and kind of energy passing through it (we will talk much more about "energy" later), and they are not all the same story.

We do know a great deal about the collapse of complex social systems, but it is somewhat like knowing the contour of a mountain from a distance, but not being able to describe well any specific portion of it.

To simplify, we can say that **a social system collapses when it doesn't have enough energy to deal with problems which arise**, both internally, like struggles between elites in a country, or externally, like changing climate or attack from enemies. We can, though, know many general traits, and can discuss them in that way.

All collapses have certain things in common, mostly that life becomes local, cities decline and life expectancy at birth declines.

Collapse has been my primary subject of study for the last 12 years. Information in this guide is derived not just from complex biocultural sociology, but history and archaeology, evolution and physics. The collapse of a complex social system, a city-state, a kingdom, an empire, shares these features:

1. A **decline in geopolitical influence**, as is reflected by trade and trade networks; a decline in social organization and specialized division of labor; locally, this means many things become unavailable.

2. **A decline in population.** This is because a complex society organizes the energy of food and other resources, and so organizes humans, and grows as they live and multiply. When there is not enough food, people die.

3. **A decline in the number and influence of cities**.

4. Often, **a decline in literacy,** writing, and keeping records and historical narratives. This is because the system can no longer afford bureaucracy.

5. **A general reduction of life expectancy at birth** (for the non-slave portion of the population). This is caused by a reduction in food and hunger, every injury might lead to tetanus or septicemia, mothers work harder and eat less so pregnancies are hard and often unsuccessful, babies die early from many causes, the old die, taking with them generational knowledge.

Every collapse is different; they take differing amounts of time to play out, and have differing consequences, but generally, they share those traits.

In our discussion, we need to keep in mind that **societal collapse plays out like a mud flow on a steep hill. Sometimes it all slowly moves, but more often some areas move slowly and others more rapidly, but all are subject, either locally or as a whole, to sudden downward changes**. (Please read that again, it's important.)

The cause of all collapse is the decline in energy, the reasons for those declines are somewhat different.
Climate change is the single biggest cause for collapse. People

need food, they need to travel, and when the climate changes, those things become easier, or more difficult.

Our numbers swelled with the advent of the Holocene[2], which was a period of warm, stable climate beginning about 12,000 years ago, and ending recently with the Anthropocene. We can think of the warm, stable weather as energy.

It is uncommon in our planet's history for the weather to be so mild, and above all, stable. Stable weather allows for agriculture, and food is energy. Lack of food is collapse.

Cities and empires arose, in the Middle East, for example, when the weather warmed after the last ice age. The warming weather melted glaciers in the mountains, and more water fell as rain instead of snow, and so rivers were born, and wetlands that were rich in wild grains, fish, and animals.

However, as those glaciers disappeared, so did the rivers, and societies died. In some instances, empires were built on trading, and the mouths of river harbors from which their ships sailed. However, they cut down the trees in the mountains to build their ships, and as a result, precipitation fell on bare slopes, and the pattern of rain changed, and the mud and sand from erosion swept down the rivers, silting up the harbors and making trade impossible.

Sometimes collapse was the result of armies, sweeping down from the steppes, for example: the Huns, the Seljuk Turks, the Mongols. Even those were caused by climate change, as rich years caused steppe populations to grow, and poor years sent them sweeping down to conquer. This teaches us two lessons: first, **weather makes all history**, and second, **there is no social force more dangerous than a mass of young people with nothing to lose.**

All Complex Societies Collapse.

They appear, sometimes they grow, occasionally becoming very large, and then, they die. Most often, when they die, they retain some life in the main cities, and along established roads and routes. But, not always.

Several factors influence how badly a system collapses. The first is the presence of other, functional systems within trading distance. The level of depletion of natural resources helps determine how far the system collapses. Epidemics, and war, can speed collapse.

There have been two significant collapses within living memory: the British empire, and the Soviet Union.

The British empire dissolved because Britain was depleted after two world wars, but mostly because the complexity, meaning the bureaucracy and networks, to control the colonies were using more energy than they were producing.

When the British took a colony, they siphoned everything worth having, including metals and other products of the environment, and they organized labor to create wealth. Having done that, the return was getting smaller as the effort needed to extract it was getting bigger.

The empire collapsed relatively slowly, and suffering in the core nation did not increase terrifically, given it was already coming out of WWII, and was already suffering food shortages both as a result of the war, and because they were now feeding starving Germans.

The collapse of the Soviet Union is more complex, and more dire. The various nations of the Soviet Union were struggling economically. They disbanded relatively swiftly, and the collapse devastated some of them, notably Russia and Ukraine.

Central control broke down, in part because of the severing of trade relations with other nations. Organized crime was everywhere, and did things like provide food, protection, and other services typically provided by government. They did so at the price the market would bear, and without supervision of the quality of their products.

Ukraine continues to be plagued with high level crime and corruption, and, though Russia fairly rapidly began to organize a strong central government, for awhile the life expectancy in Russia fell to that of wartime.

However, those collapses took place in a global society which still maintained busy trade networks. Britain still controls a tremendous amount of wealth, and the nations of the Soviet Union immediately began to trade with each other, and the EU.

In the late Bronze age, a collapse occurred which sent nearly every nation (North Africa and Southeast Europe, Egypt, eastern Libya, the Balkans, the Aegean, Anatolia, and the centralized societies of the Caucasus) into decline as described above, and it happened with blinding speed, and many of them never recovered as the Iron Age rose and obscured them.

But, what we care about is our collapse, so what can we tell about that?

What Will Most Likely Cause Our Collapse?

Climate change is number two, behind **number one, nuclear war** (the final finish for humankind if it happens).

We have known about the effects of CO_2 on climate since 1824 when it was described by French mathematician and physicist Joseph Fourier. The changing climate will do many things to upset the current global social system. Climate change, throughout Earth's history, often took a little more time; climate change now is happening very rapidly. It will cause people to migrate, not only to escape weather changes, but to escape food and other resources shortages, and of course, violence.

Weather makes history: often this is the history it makes.

Number three is physical energy and natural resource decline.

Here we refer to the potentially rapidly approaching point where the fossil fuels we can get are not worth what it costs to pump, transport and refine, and distribute them. There will be no magical transition, not to nuclear power, not to solar and wind. No other energy source is as portable, powerful, and versatile, as fossil fuels. Even coal and natural gas lag behind liquid petrofuels. The products of fossil fuels are all around us in plastics and other products. The other forms of energy, including hydroelectric dams, are all fossil fuel derivatives, they can't be made without oil, coal and gas.

The changing climate will put new demands on energy.

Number four is massive over population.

This includes the over eight billion people, and the incredibly long and deeply complex networks needed to feed them all, and the complexity they require. The system ceaselessly creates new context enabling more people to be born, and more to live past childhood, to reproductive age.

The rate of growth of population is diminishing; there are still far, far too many people. We consider that our global population probably was probably between 50,000 and 50 million for 300,000 years. It hit 500 million in about 1470, or, in other words, almost 10,000 years after the start of the Holocene. In the early 1800s, about 335 years later, it was a billion.

How big is a billion? If you could count one number every second and didn't stop counting once you began, it would take over 30 years. No one can do that, though, (say out loud 903,483,592; did it take longer than a second?), and people need to eat, sleep and use the facilities nearly every day. Reasonably, it would take about a hundred years to actually do.

Two billion was about 1927, 125 years later; we note that it would take longer to count to two billion that it did for the population to reach it. Three billion in 1960, 33 years later. Fourteen years later, 1974, four billion. In 1987, 13 years later, five billion. Six billion in 1999, 12 years later. Seven billion in 2011, 12 years later. And, only 11 years later, eight billion people.

We recall that, only twenty-thousand years earlier there were probably fewer than 50 million people, perhaps far fewer. We can see that the system is very good for turning natural resources into humans, but it is not an infinite planet.

Number five is the fragile state of the global social structure itself.

While some complex systems can run far from equilibrium for a long time, most can't. In the case of our global system, it is approaching a "closed environment." Up until now, abundant natural resources caused the system to act as though it were open, with new resources all the time, and endless places to dump trash and waste. But, the system has overgrown all that. It will require more energy to obtain energy, and no system can run on that forever.

The first four are factors upsetting the energy flow of the social system. It has its own requirements, and its own lifespan. The broader and more complex it becomes, the more energy it takes to organize the complexity necessary to keep running. At some point, the system hits a point of diminishing returns, and it has to sacrifice some parts of itself.

That means, that part collapses; to the inhabitants of that peripheral area (by which we mean it is distant in some way from the urban core of the system) it is a collapse: lifespan decreases, people leave, and writing and reading cease to be everyday necessities.

After a significant loss of such peripheral subsystems, the core of the system itself begins to fray. The decline can be prolonged, as it was for Rome (which, by some estimations took several centuries including the Eastern Roman, or Byzantine empire), or it can be sudden.

It depends entirely on how energy runs through the system.

What is key here is that every family comes away with an understanding of what it is that is collapsing, and why, the nature of it. It is the social system, which, without anyone doing anything to control it, organizes humans, and other forms of energy, through extended networks. It turns natural resources into humans, and uses energy in the process, because energy is life for the system, and for every family.

As this declines, or collapses, those networks fail.

For every family in collapse, it means getting used to bad news.

3. THE THREE INTERTWINED FORMS OF ENERGY

One of the central ideas so far has been that a complex system organizes energy. We have referred to the start of the Holocene as a point where weather energy turned in our favor, and we have discussed the importance of physical energy to the system.

The most useful definition of energy is that it makes things happen, it does work.

Physical Energy

It is easy to see how physical energy like coal or wind or food, do work, they move and heat and cool our world. Human energy, in the sense of laborers and slaves, did much physical work even before the Holocene.

More subtle, though, is the nature of human energy to the system.

Human Energy

The predictions and determinations you make with other humans, individuals or groups, will likely be the most frequent, and most critical. In this section we very briefly describe humans, how they function, and how their ceaseless interaction continues complex systems.

Human energy is more than labor output, it is humans doing things, in particular, doing things in a regularized way. This is the power that organizes all human societies. In a technical sense, humans are the medium through which the system organizes energy. However, that is not really how we sense society.

It would be very useful to predict what people will do, and indeed, doing so consumes much of our lives. However, in a more general sense, it would be important to know what groups of people would be likely to do. If we consider joining other families, or taking a side, or going to war, we want to know what others are likely to do. Governments and marketing agencies spend a great deal of effort on this. We will not be able to duplicate their results.

But, we can still collect information, use the information, understanding what it means in the larger society, and perhaps reduce the likelihood of misfortune.

Humans are simple, and have a relatively few choices in what they do. But, it is this simplicity, played out in social context, that allows for social organization and complexity. So, even though we can speak about humans being simple, we still can't easily and reliably predict what people will do. Those who work for corporations and governments work very hard to determine what people will do.

We sense ourselves and those around us as sincerely taking part in life. We hope for good things, fear bad things, work towards taking care of ourselves and those we care about to the best of our ability, given the situation.

The social world seems seamless; wherever we look, there is it. It is also mostly transparent, we really aren't aware of it that much. In a way, we have little idea of the work that we, and other people do in the world. To explain, I will describe humans simply.

We are long lived, highly social animals. In general, we share propensities. Not all humans evidence all the propensities, and most humans don't evidence them all the time. Most people do, most of the time, and that is what keeps the social world going.

By contrast, if we were all like bears, for example, and social only some times of the year, there would be no cities, no any human culture.

Our Propensities Are:

1. **We want to live**. If we don't want to live, we die and disappear from society. Some people desperately want to live; others live as an action of habit and expectation, but nearly all people show the trait of wanting to live. That gives people tremendous motivation to take actions to stay alive. We can assume that most of the people reading this are doing so because they want to stay alive in hard times.

2. **We want our family and friends to live.** This is sensible for three reasons. First, because we care about them. Next, because they are our social support group, they increase our influence in the social world. Finally, because we can't help it, humans are extremely social, and, indeed, some biologists[3] have suggested we are eusocial, like bees and ants. Very few humans can live without some contact with other humans. Affiliation, the need to do things with others, is paramount in our species, it is why we join churches and political parties and support football teams.

3. **We want the regard of our society, and especially our peers.** This means we want them to think well of us. This is about status, and status refers to the legitimacy and authority of our claim to the welfare, the surplus, of society. If we are citizens in good standing, we are treated better than if we are despised by those we associate with.

4.   In general, we associate with those with whom we share **similarity, familiarity and proximity**. **We want what we perceive others of our status have, known as "relative deprivation."** This is a natural strategy, which causes us, in general, to want whatever others in our social group have. But, it generally prevents us from eating the rich, or rather, from demanding what those outside our social group have. It cements us in our social group, and makes social stratification, or the differentiation of social class. It is why we have hierarchy. Similarity, familiarity, and proximity.

We see that, though there is certainly variation, human propensities are all about status, or the legitimacy and authority to control the surplus of the society. From the lowliest to the bloated elite, each tends to follow those essential propensities. Not everyone, and not always for anyone, but for enough of us, enough of the time. It is enough to keep a complex society going.

Those behavioral tendencies play out to become everything we know about the social world, and define our relationship with others.

Humans Are Contextual Beings

We are who we are in context, in the social surroundings. Humans, even when planning for the future or remembering some past event, are only ever now. They remember the past now; they imagine the future by imposing now on some imagined time.

This is not to diminish memories, or plans for the future; they are essential, we can't do without them. Even so, we have to remember that, even though we try be otherwise, we do it now, because of the context of what we do.

Consider how this works in everyday life, through these brief scenarios:

1. *Driving on a crowded street, you see a policeman in uniform. He waves you to the side of the road, and you pull over.*

Why did he pull you over? You worry, did you break a law you didn't know about? You try not to look nervous, or "guilty."

Why did you pull over? He was indicating his legitimacy and authority to cause you to behave a certain way. He wore a uniform. He had a badge, and identification. He spoke as though he expected to be obeyed. Others on the street treated him with deference.

Your legitimacy and authority to drive a car can be impacted by this person, and what he represents. Or, if you are carrying highly illegal cargo, you might try to fight or run, and be killed. That is how real the idea of status is for us.

2. *You are walking on a quiet street just before dark. Someone is coming towards you on the same sidewalk.*

From as far as possible, and probably without thinking about it, you gather information about them: gender, age, health, attractiveness, social status, and perhaps intent.

Do you know them? Do they look at you for some time, or just glance and look away? Do they alter their course toward or away from your course? You know the acceptable, and unacceptable, possible outcomes.

I have avoided reference to authors because this is a short work, and the reader likely doesn't care, (there is a list of sources at the end of the book), but here I refer to Dorothy and W.I. Thomas, who said, **"If people define situations as real, they are real in their consequences."** This simple observation describes all of the social world.

To maintain our status, we dress, speak, and act to the status we hold, or want to hold. In sociology, dramaturgy is the description of the rituals and roles we use to organize society.

We sometimes think rituals are something people do in religious events, maybe in other places, but no, "ritual" means the choreographed, socially agreed upon things we constantly do to keep society together in our little corners.

We have "scripts" for our part. If our role is mother, we know what that means in our society, what behaviors it implies, what benefits it should entitle a mother to, and so on.

However, no one has just one role, do they? Policeman is a role: it implies dress and identification, a publicly state goal (to prevent crime and keep the peace), and language which we consider ritual language, "Statute 12277, subsection 449b;" "keep your hands where I can see them;" "lay face down on the ground with your arms spread out and your palms up." These are not everyday words.

We have other roles, too, perhaps "Lutheran", or "Yankee fan", or "Democrat". All have their special roles, and some require us to hate others. Sometimes the roles are forced to clash, when a social situation requires us to have two opposing roles: "Mom" and "cheating spouse" for example.

Our roles tell us what to expect of the world and ourselves, and they provide an important means, a way of being, which helps us decipher the social information we get from everyday life.

It is a feature which regularizes the status of each role, and allows a person to accrue status from different sources. It provides a way of keeping us socially connected, and of connecting our little corner of the system.

Just the act of walking on the sidewalk towards someone involves a series of judgments and decisions, and a kind of ritual once you pass. Depending on your assessments on the approach, you might smile and talk, or wave, or just nod, or look ahead and "not see" them, or you might cross the street before they reach you.

You might forget the moment at once, or something about the interaction might linger: perhaps they are attractive; perhaps they are unsettling; perhaps they remind you of someone. You will probably forget the event, or perhaps you might talk with someone, and let them know the person was in the neighborhood.

You will make many assumptions based on how the person looks, and many of them will be wrong, because the assumptions are less about the other person than they are about you, and how the person made you feel.

However, many of them will be right. This is because, first of all, we are all very much alike, even though the differences between us are what we care about socially. Being much alike, we are able to guess what others might be thinking.

We can also weigh the behavior of others through those social clues of status, and of the organizing system we each fit in to in society. How much can we bring to a social interaction?

We have a personal value, for example, our value as a mate, or as an ally, and a status value. Things about us which help locate us in social space are things like attractiveness or fertility, relations and networks, and wealth. We negotiate that value in every interaction.

We Create Logical Narratives, For Ourselves, And Others

When we all recognize those narratives, they are real in their consequences, even if we disagree with the premise of them. We all "nuance" our narratives, encouraging others to accept our description of a social "truth."

An easily seen example is someone running for political office. They and their staff work hard to portray the candidate as honest, trustworthy, genuinely concerned, and holding values they will stand by.

Sometimes, we believe the narrative, sometimes we don't, because, intuitively as social beings, we know that we can be manipulated by the truth claims of others.

When we talk about similarity, familiarity and proximity, those are the things we refer to: where do you fit, what is your value, in social space. If I see you often, so we are close to each other, we have familiarity and proximity; if we share important views, then we have similarity.

When we make our assessments of others, even simply walking down the street, we use all our knowledge, from our innate understanding of our kind, to our understanding of social cues about status, and our evaluation of the immediate circumstance, from mass actions with thousands of others, to individuals passing on the street.

What we feel is everything. This is because all the unconscious estimating and figuring we do often does not produce rational thought. What it produces is emotion, and emotion is what we remember after an interaction.

We simply don't have memory storage sufficient to store every interaction, but our emotions are easily summed, and easily stored in association with a person, a group, or even a place.

The names of emotions and what we call them is partly based on custom, **but they always reflect some aspect of a necessity of life, and all are about status, which is access to the surplus of society**.

In the West, and elsewhere, there is a rough agreement that the basic emotions are these:

Affiliation: *We have to network with other people to live*. There are humans who have little or relatively no social network, but they often do not thrive. For humans, affiliation is how we orchestrate our status. It allows us to have varying status, so we might be despised as a father but successful at law. More affiliation means more reliable networks.

We know what affiliation feels like. We get it, perhaps, in church. Perhaps from watching a sporting even, our side against their side. We get it when we are included in family activities, and take part in key rituals in their lives: graduation from school; marriage, and so on. The event itself might see small gains or losses in statues, but not much, and the pleasant buzz of doing things with other people compensates.

Affiliation is the foundation for other social emotions, like trust. **Trust** means confidence in reciprocity, the energy invested will be returned. It means the outcome is expected to be predictable. Affiliation has one feeling, and being left out, a different one.

Love/affection: When we experience love or affection, including non physical indications of bonding between, for example, heterosexual males, a flood of endorphins in the brain gives a pleasurable feeling and memory. There is an evolutionary advantage to this, and all emotions. In this instance, it causes people to bond, increasing their likelihood of survival, and so, that of their family.

Hate: this is a very powerful personal and social emotion, it binds individuals and nations. It is an emotion which favors survival. The narratives on hatred vary, but it is essentially recognition of some struggle for status or resources directly.

If you cheat me and I hate you, I not only avoid further interaction, but I help create a social loss for you by reducing your support group, since I am motivated to tell others of your treachery.

If my people hate your people, we have a powerful bond among ourselves in our hatred of you. If you represent a threat to our status or access to resources, we can try to kill you, in preference to competition within the group where we kill each other.

Hate is a manifestation of jealousy, which is a feature of relative deprivation, believing we should have something that someone else has, or threatens. Resentment can be enduring, for generations.

Also part of the "hate group" of emotions, is revenge. Or, call it justice. This is resentment for a loss, and it seeks direct action to either recover the loss, or extract a similar loss from the other party.

As a form of "self help," revenge is the last effort to correct the wrong. It means some kind of individual or group action to try to shift the loss. Revenge killings between two or more groups can decimate a generation, or perhaps, lead to nuclear war.

As noted, hate is an emotion that spawns other emotions.

Guilt is fear of discovery of a transgression, or a crime, which can be anything which would decrease a person's legitimacy, and so status. For any interaction which is forbidden or denigrated by the social structure, discovery means loss.

Shame is the effect of that loss. Shame can include prison, the record of which makes getting a legitimate job difficult. Or it could mean the loss of faith of the community generally, making it hard to find a social network. However, shame can also help form new social peers, but of our own new status. Shame is expressed as degradation.

Degradation. This is the society wide devaluation of a person or group. It has a "feeling," and it is not a comforting one. The more a person or group of people are disconnected from the flows of energy (which make life pleasant and somewhat longer), the more likely their lives are to be shorter and more difficult.

Here we repeat a caution already mentioned: *people with nothing to lose, especially in large numbers, are very dangerous.* When a person, or group of people, are denied legitimate authority to access the surplus of society, they dis-invest in that society, and invest in the those like themselves.

Pride, hubris. This is a very powerful affiliative emotion. It references shared values and strengthens individual and group bonds. It can also encourage risk taking. We can see the evolutionary advantage here and how it relates to status.

Longing, curiosity and wanderlust are also emotions people feel. We are curious monkeys, with extraordinarily long legs, who have often lived by wandering and exploring.

This emotion confers an evolutionary benefit because, first of all, those members of the group who tend to know people in distant places increase the likelihood of cooperation with distant neighbors, by which we mean neighbors not in direct competition with us.

People who travel set the figurative and even literal pathways for networks to form. People who leave the group tend to add variation to the gene pool. Variation means an increased chance of resistance to disease and adversity; it is also known as "hybrid vigor."

People who leave the group reduce pressure on local resources. Not everyone has wanderlust, but nearly everyone has some yearning, which motivates them to take risks to achieve a hopefully improved situation.

We see these traits in monkeys, and squirrels, and all kinds of animals. Life is a struggle for energy, for food. Each individual has to earn energy for the day, and if they are to reproduce, they need even more energy yet.

Life is dangerous, because, just as we seek energy, we represent a meal for someone else. We have to be able to go far enough to find new resources, but not so far that we become food. That is the way of life for most animals, and for many people, as well.

Basic human behavior is not that difficult to understand; people act in rational ways, to live, have those they have invested in live, and to do this, they need affiliation, networking and so, status, which determines their legitimate share of the social surplus.

The range of emotions, the manner in which we can nuance several emotions at once, influenced by the chemistry of the body itself, can play out in an amazing array of behaviors. People are complex.

Actually predicting what any person or group will do is difficult. **The more you understand the person or group, against the notion of "status", or access to the surplus of society, the more easily you can predict, or imagine, what they think the choices are**. These will probably be the most important predictions you can make.

We can take this away: **the most stable networks your family forms will likely be with people who have about as much to gain or lose as your family does.**

We still have an important, but difficult to fully conceptualize, form of energy left: debt, or money. In every sense, debt is a human behavior, and we might insist it is a form of human energy, since debt and money are nothing, except when humans make them real in their consequences.

Debt Energy; Money Is Time

In a relatively few thousand years the system has developed debt from shaped wads of clay with a specific number of pebbles in it, representing that number of sheep, for example, to bits of information on a global computer network.

Key to our discussion of decline and collapse, the time might come again when clay is worth more than plastic money.

Energy makes things happen, it does work, makes things move. In the modern world, and **for the last five thousand years, debt energy has made things happen.**

Your family might already understand the nature of debt, but let's take a long view of it, because it is possible the future might look like the past. If the power goes out, all over the world, those computer dollars disappear.

As mentioned, it is possible that one early form of debt, or money, was a specifically shaped piece of clay, with pebbles in it. Some were found; does that mean they were money? No, but we can test the idea that debt is a powerful force by considering what it does.

If, in public, I give you a clay shape, it means I owe you six sheep, or whatever. I take whatever I wanted from you, and promise you six sheep down the road. When you get the sheep, we break the shape.

We have concluded a deal over something that is not present, and might not even have been born yet. We have made **a solid symbol of the idea of time and distance**.

We have, by mutual agreement, and through the emotions of affiliation, agreed to trust. Debt assumes repayment, but the uncertainty of the future is a cost.

The uncertainty has led to compound interest, and insurance, and tax schemes. But, the power of debt is still considerable.

Included in this discussion of debt as energy, we will finally discuss "networks," "nexuses," and "nodes."

There were networks before there was formalized debt. In truth, debt is an extension of the expectation people have that status support will be repaid. Or, physical support.

If a friend is in trouble, you may, at some risk or cost to yourself, help them. You do it on the basis of your familiarity, and on the belief that if you needed the favor repaid, it would be.

That is the start of little clay shapes, and the basis of the powerful money control center in the town of London proper, which has massive influence on the global economy.

Humans often wander, in particular inclined persons, and in the course of wandering, they exchange favors. There was trade before money, some of it quite long distance. A wanderer might buy amber at the Baltic Sea at a low exchange rate and trade it elsewhere at an inflated value, in trade for silver at a low price there.

But, money made everything much easier. It had a value for anything, not just specified livestock. It didn't die, and could be accumulated.

It made trade so much easier. It also made taxing easier. We know there were trade routes in Asia and Europe 40,000 years ago; however, about five thousand years ago trade really took off.

The trade routes are the roads and rivers and ports; those are the physical aspect of a network. However, the exchange of energy in a network takes place where people are, doing what people do, where they buy and sell.

Money made trade networks grow and extend. Those networks that had nexuses, meaning towns and cities spaced to attract traders to stay, and spend a little money, and make some good deals, expanded; urban centers grew and attracted more networks, until some became nexuses of global trade.

To help us understand the significance of networks, we consider these illustrations.

First is Singapore, a tiny state on the tip of the Malay Peninsula. With only 283 square miles of land, it is the second most densely populated place on the planet, with 5.6 million people. It also has the fourth largest port in Southeast Asia, and among the busiest globally. This is why it has the third highest standard of living in the world.

Its position in the physical world, at the tip of Malay, with a confluence of ocean trade routes, attracts foreign investment to build infrastructure. The state is also heavily into finance, drawing huge surplus from handling debt energy.

But, Singapore is important in our discussion of collapse because of its vulnerability. First, the massive wealth there comes from burning fossil fuels. That cheap physical energy is converted to debt and human energy in Singapore, but as energy availability declines all ports will suffer.

Further, most of the urban part of the island is less than 50 feet above sea level. The same features which make it attractive to shipping also subject it to significant weather events and sea level rise.

Next, are two photos of cities at night. The lights trace out the networks and even hint at the rate of flow on each.

First is Houston[4]:

Then, Tokyo[5]

We can see from these examples how important the nexuses of cities are.

From the time of the first true cities, the function of the city was to gather energy. One way that works is to have the savages in the mountains bring you timber and tin in exchange for cheap goods. If a city needed to, it could arm men and force outlying areas to be productive.

Again, in the first cities, humans were monetized, given a value as slaves. Slaves powered cities; in Athens and Rome, up to 30% of the population were slaves. Rome, in one period, for example, was a cesspit of death, and slaves were constantly imported to maintain the population.

So, the value of a human was reduced to cash. That is the power of debt. It moves people from place to place, and makes it possible to harvest the surplus of rural and distant areas of their natural resources, and even their people.

The health of a network is reflected in the flow of energy it carries. **The health of a nexus is the quantity and value of energy it distributes and collects.**

Archaeologists, when considering the collapse and regeneration of the early social structures, from about 3,000 BC, talk about "decentralization" and "re-centralization" or "reurbanization;" those networks, and the nexuses of cities, is what they were referring to.

It is important to us when we do our calculations, and make our guesses on how the reliability of resources we need will be, to **remember the idea of flow**. What networks, meaning both roads and sources of goods, can you rely on?

For that matter, what kind of money can you rely on?

We recall that powerful cities have died because ports silted up or trade routes changed. When the system is healthy, those networks bring the city all it needs to maintain itself, to feed and house its people.

However, when incoming energy flows decline, the cities begins to die. People leave, or become more predatory, and sometimes it declines or collapses.

It is significant that the three types of energy are not interchangeable, but can be substituted. If you have a great deal of human energy, it will substitute for other kinds of physical energy. If you have a great deal of debt energy, it will buy other kinds of energy.

But, the exchange is not free, when using a less efficient form of energy to accomplish a task, there is a net energy loss over the maximized energy source.

For example, the primary energy source for humans is food. As I write this, in the West, there is an abundance of food. Some people do go hungry, but few are hungry all the time.

However, for most animals, and for humans outside of complex societies, hunger is a near constant state, punctuated by brief periods of plenty. There are generally, on a healthy Earth, seasons of plenty and seasons of want, but most often, getting food energy takes physical energy, and for human subsistence farmers, even debt energy.

When we think about food shortages, we have to think about other factors which are influenced by it. Sometimes, social unrest accompanies shortages. Food shortages can mean labor shortages, because people need to eat to work. Our family, and our global system, can only store so much food.

We are far too many for everyone to grow or gather their own food, and those who try to grow their own food often fail, because it is not easy.

Growing food (there will be no hunting, all animals that can be eaten will be killed by rural huger) is an art, composed of doing hard work efficiently, and understanding soil and seed. Even then, in the best of weather seasons, it is not easy. We will not often have reliable weather, as the climate changes.

In a famine, people will do anything for food, and will eat anything. The stark truth is, when the networks which bring us our food fail, human life will be cheap.

We can see that storing freeze dried food is not enough. We have to be able to identify the networks that bring us food, and expect them to get shorter. We have to expect to pay a premium price for small amounts of a limited variety of food. In a true famine, there will be almost no food.

How durable are our networks for food? How do we identify and anticipate the reliability of networks?

That is a question of methodology.

4. METHODOLOGY: HOW TO FIGURE THE ODDS

Gather data.
Turn it into information:
>**Evaluate it for reliability and then pertinence**
>**Classify it in relation to the priority groups**
>**Store and protect it**
>**Manipulate it**

Having a general understanding of humans, and how and why we join together to create complex societies, how do we use that to help predict the likelihood of on-coming changes?

We Gather Data

Then we evaluate it for source and reliability, and determine what value it will have. By "value," we mean we apply our priorities: how likely is the information, what source and reliability; how does it effect our well being; how will we weigh it against other information.

Then classify it, meaning we decide where it applies in our estimations, and to which of our concerns.

Then it is recorded, or filed, where it will be available for us to consider when making a guess about the future.

We have only so much energy to devote to the project of prediction; the immediacy of life can make the future less important. We have only so much space to store information. We have only so much expertise at organizing and manipulating data. Even so, any understanding of data and what it represents will give us an edge on preparing for what might come next.

Whatever approach we use, we first need data. **We need real world estimates of a number of things, variables.**

We use the term "variable" to mean that it is something we can calculate or test for. We don't have to use that term, but we need some word that means "the things we are considering in relationship to each other."

The benefit of using the term is that being a variable isn't a feature of the thing, it is a feature of how we look at it. Anything can be a variable, meaning we can gather data, track, and manipulate it.

Manipulating the data can certainly mean doing mathematical tests to determine the likely accuracy of our guess. It depends on how much your family wants to invest in the work of it.

Methods of using information come in many forms, some of which are good at describing short term changes, and others which have a broader implication, or help us see changes several layers or many networks from us.

What happens in the federal government is always important, for example, but because all we really have are truth claims, we can't be sure what version of the truth to believe.

It might help to understand in terms of actual rises and declines in the value and trading percentages of certain networks, what the state of the nation really is. What is the jobless rate; what is the rate of people no longer looking for jobs, what percent of those under the poverty level have jobs that don't pay enough. All of these are measures of how well the economy is doing, and that is information which can be fairly easily, at this time, found on the internet.

However, sometimes that information is either unavailable or untrustworthy. In that case, we need to "interpolate," which means to "guess," using what information we do have to help fill in for the information we need.

It works like this: we would like to know the price of gas on a certain date this year, but we don't have that information. We do have information for that date last year, and we can compare them to the data from this year. If we consider them together, we can see how the over all prices last year compare to this year, and make a guess about what the price was this year based on last year's trend. "Trend" means "the general direction of the data," or where things seem to be going.

We have to be realistic: corporations and governments spend a huge effort to gather data, sift it for reliability, catalog it, use it to form a large picture of whatever they want to know. We can't do that.

However, there is a diminishing return on data. The first fifteen facts you learn about different aspects of the network, or the reliability of people, are potentially worth much more than the last 25 facts you learn (provided they are not changes in status, only in depth of analysis, or number of layers of networks).

It is difficult to have enough data, but sometimes the data we have can suffice. Sometimes we just can't organize more data.

Bad data, or data we misinterpret, is very serious when you have only a small amount to work with, but sometimes we use what we have.

Sources Have Value According To Their Reliability

Eye witness and self report data is the least valuable. We already know why: people have their own narratives, and always present themselves in the things they say.

Much better is to use hard data. How many people are doing this or that behavior, visiting the store, or going to a bar. How crowded is the bus at key times; where are people going. What items are going up in price, and what are going down, or staying stable. When there is a shortage of a commodity, how long does the shortage last. When there is a shortage of a preferred commodity, then usually people select the next best thing: how is the supply of those substitute items holding up?

It can't be stressed enough: collect data, gather information, notice things in the society around you.

Having said that, there are many problems with actually doing that. In part, because data and information are not exactly the same thing. Data is a fact: the price of beef has doubled in four months. It becomes information when we use it in some context, some logical way of arranging data.

So, let's use the fact that the price of beef has doubled in four months. It would be nice to have the full data set, meaning every trip to the supermarket, note the price of the same cut of beef. Saying it has doubled in four months could mean it was lower for awhile, then returned to normal, then doubled in three weeks.

See how that is: "in four months" covers a lot of change, and likely it slowly increased in price, but almost certainly, not evenly. Knowing the stability of the price is very important to knowing what the influences might be on the networks that bring us beef. We will do that with a time series chart, later on.

Let's consider things that would increase the price of beef, and think how they fit in to the price we see, and where we think the price of beef might go.

First, might be the strength of your currency. In other words, the debt energy. Is everything in the market going up by about the same amount? A completely across the board change in prices indicates the value of the currency is decreasing, so more dollars are needed to buy the same cart of groceries. That is most likely going to change gradually.

If the meat comes from a long way off, and the price increases are not uniform on all products, the price of diesel is going up. Cross reference the cost of beef with the cost of gasoline and particularly diesel, at the pump.

It could mean a bad year for corn or soy, and feed costs were higher. It could mean an outbreak of a bovine disease. It could be that your beef came from some other nation, and trade agreements have broken down. It could mean lenders were unwilling to create debt for farmers who can only pay so much interest, and so no feed.

We can't know all the reasons, but we can find out what we can, because it tells us something about the way the three forms of energy are flowing. Meantime track beef as a variable, but eat beans and rice.

So, we can see that, to make an intelligent guess at what will happen, we need data available in a useful way, and have a plan against which we can turn data into information.

How do we do this, exactly? It depends on your resources, the amount of energy you have available to put into the problem.

We likely need to emulate bureaucrats down through the ages, and have a way of writing data down. Computers allow us to run programs and store huge amounts of data, but they break down, or the power goes off. Paper is cumbersome, difficult to rearrange or add or subtract items.

Your data has value, it represents energy invested in the future, and it needs to be protected; encryption and passwords on the computer, and a tight container and an out of the way place for the paper. A prudent person might do the work on computer when it is possible, but print off periodic copies with spaces for annotation.

We note here that some data is **quantifiable**, meaning it is numbers or easily turned into numbers. A lot of our best data, though is about **qualities**.

We can try to quantify them: these beans are better than those beans. How much better? We can force a number: on a scale of one to ten, how much better. However that quantity won't contain valuable information about why one was better. Critical data can be lost that way.

We can see that if we change or specify the definition of "better," we can fine tune our quantifying a quality: this bean tastes better, this bean has more energy. This bean will grow when others will not. If we break that into three values, so we can determine which we prefer (taste, energy, and reliability), we can weight those values and determine which bean to grow the most of.

Note: grow some of all three; in a good year you can sell the tasty beans at a profit and perhaps use the money for rice or meat, and eat the other two beans together.

Organize your data anyway you like, but I propose you do so by source. Within each source, organize by priority group. Choose the priorities you want to, but generally they are those things necessary for living: Food and Water; Shelter; Transportation; Security; Community (FWSTSC).

Sources Might Be:

Official news is usually not very accurate, but it alerts you to the fact that something is happening, or at least some version of what is happening. It is useful for longer range planning, either farther in the future, or a greater distance away. Organize by priority group (FWSTSC, or whatever priority group you choose). Don't forget, governments and corporations create narratives.

First hand information organized by priority group. This includes the price and availability of food, the safety of the shelter, transportation cost and reliability, and so on. These are reliable facts, and something easily quantified.

Hearsay, by reliability of source. This requires us to give a number to a quality. How reliable is the source? Maybe one source would be more reliable in one exchange, if they are close to the original source, or that is their specialty, but lower in another, because they are just repeating gossip. Don't forget people create narratives.

At The End Of The Day, The Family Should Debrief

That means to share what they have learned during the day, with someone noting the data for later entry, or directly entering the data. The family could discuss the reliability and pertinence of data.

Having all the family working on the project is key, because **the debriefing and discussion help unify the group and get everyone up to speed**. Besides, gathering and organizing data is a big task, and everyone is probably needed.

We know we have limited energy to spend on this project. We likely have the most time to spend on it when we need it the least, when things are going well. That needs to be a measure you keep, how much energy you steal from doing data to do more pressing things, because it is a measure of how much energy you have available to the family. See?

There are very real limits to the data you can harvest, and much of it seems to go nowhere. With a computer and artificial intelligence, it is possible to pick out patterns in data which an unaided human will probably miss, especially one who has spent the day working.

You have an advantage which helps balance the lack of all that energy to spend. You were born into the world, are of the world, and you know how it works innately.

If your family has someone who likes to arrange data, and have their finger on the pulse, let them record and organize the information, as well as the source data, from the family discussion. It would ideally be organized by date and by subject. Time is an important factor in determining how likely and when, something might happen.

If you can spare the person, and they do well at it, pay them for their time by shifting other tasks to someone else, or by some other affordable compensation. Your data, and the ability to turn it into information, can be a valuable tool in the kit your family needs to survive.

If you don't have the energy to do all that, get a pad of paper, put down the date and record all the information the family has. It can be organized later if you have the time; if not, at least you have a record to look back on, and to note, for example, increases and decreases in the variables which most effect our survival.

Data into information:

We understand that people go to college for years to learn to turn data into information. As with everything about this process, it is complex, and so likely to be inherently difficult.

In this instance it is because data itself should be neutral. It is a record of something that happened, to the best of our knowledge. Translating that into something we can use requires us to have methodology, or ways of doing things logically. That, in turn, requires us to make value decisions.

Once we do that, inevitably, we frame what we can know from

the data, because we have determined the criteria, that is the definitions and values of the variables are represented in the qualifying of the variables.   We have decided what each one "means" to us.

We did it with beans: taste, nutrition, reliability. What was the source of our data? We all ate the beans and know one is more appealing, and a second is filling and sticks to our ribs, and our bean crew report, and demonstrate with quantity, the third is most reliable. We can prioritize issues and give each a relative value.

A **"relative value" means we have quantified a quality based on how important it is to us, and relative to the other facts we have**, both on that subject or priority group, but also by type of event or information. A riot downtown, for example, means unrest, but also difficulty with travel, perhaps. If it is a food riot, it has pertinence to food, as well, as a priority.

We still have to find ways to quantify qualities. Most people are familiar with "on a scale of one to five" or "on a scale of one to ten." It is about the quickest way to quantify data. However, with the beans, we would have three characteristics; lets have a scale for taste, energy, and reliability.

We can average them and get a value for each bean.   BUT, important information is missing.

If we plant all delicious beans, and the weather turns against us, we will starve because they will not grow. If we plant delicious beans and have to work very hard, we will eat more of those beans than we would the most nutritious bean, and will have to plant more beans. If we plant the resilient bean, we are less likely to starve, but we will have to grow more beans than the nutritious bean (which might not be difficult, since it is resilient, but we still have to spend energy clearing land to do so).

We have to be arbitrary, and make an educated guess, and ask ourselves, which of the three characteristics is most important? In good times, it might be tasty beans. In uncertain weather, it might well be resilient beans.

In that case, we say: we place a greater value on resilience, and so we add a point to those beans. We find the family likes tasty beans, and rate them highly on the scale; those beans might get an over all value (on 1-5) of 4. Energy rich beans get a 3. Resilient beans get a 3, but we weight them to a 4.

We still have to decide between two four-rated beans; it would have been easier, when writing this, to simply give tasty beans a 3, so weighting the resilient beans would mean they win; in real life, we have to chose between variables which are rated about the same, so decide yourself: tasty beans, or hardscrabble beans!

It is more difficult to give values to other important issues, like that the bus did eventually arrive, but it was already full. The bus did arrive but it was crammed and it took a long, more wandering route now, which delayed us more than an hour. The bus did arrive and it was crowded, and young men with guns robbed everyone, so they had nothing to give the robbers at the bus stop. Whatever the nature of the information is.

How do we enter information like that?

We could actually do so across several variables, from reliability (how often does it arrive, how often too full to get a seat) and efficiency (might have walked in 45 minutes instead), and, in this instance, safety. We could weight them as safety, efficiency, and reliability, noting that if the bus does not come at all, or we cannot get a seat, there is a cost to that, as well.

If we can't use the bus, we might have to call in a favor, or pay a higher cost, or take greater risks. Those are all things we care about, and need to help our family understand, prepare for, and survive.

And often so much is at stake, that we can't help but be emotionally involved. **Even so, when considering the data and creating information, we need to be, what? Dispassionate.**

Cost Benefit Analysis

Many times, we can do a "cost-benefit analysis" (c/b) as a way of capturing how much energy we lose or gain on an event. Have a family meeting on such an important issue, and discuss the likely loss or gain on any risk taken.

But, c/b has to include a discussion of "**what if this happens,** what will we do; what if it does not happen, what will we do. What will be the consequences, the gain or loss of resources, family well being, if this happens, **or if it does not happen**?"

If we catch a bus we can get a seat on which will take a relatively short route, what do we gain or lose. What if we wait for two uncertain buses to get a seat on a subsequent bus (figuring efficiency and safety), what will the ultimate loss be? What is our alternative plan?

Some Ways To Organize Information

One of the simplest and most useful ways to organize data is the "time series." These simply take a value (qualitative data works best) and record it on a graph over time.

Below is a time series of the US total receipts[6]:

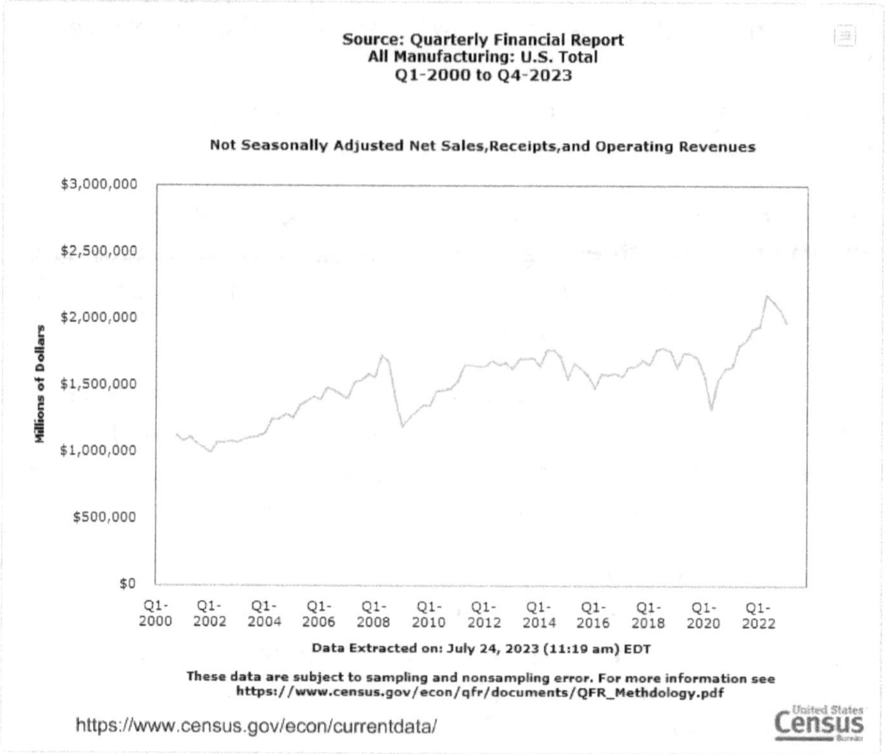

Looking at the graph, we see it is something, dollars figured on the one "axis," going up, and time on the other. There are some interesting patterns on this graph, but our graph of the price of meat would not look like that.

Further, the amount in dollars is not adjusted for inflation, and so, it looks like the US is doing well, but perhaps it is not, because more dollars which are worth less does not mean more energy is flowing through the economy.

In a time series graph, the length of time, and the interval of time are two different things, and they show different things.

The graph of the economy is taken on the same day each year. We don't see the economy going up and down as we would if we saw it change every day. A shorter interval allows increased "detail," but it also means more data gathering and record keeping.

A time period on a graph which is too short means there isn't enough activity to form patterns; we haven't been recording data long enough to see what changes in energy happen under different circumstances. So a time period of less than a year won't show seasonal changes, for example.

Ideally, our graphs all have the same interval and time period, so we can most easily look for trends across our variables.

We can expect that, even in a decline and collapse, some things will get better, perhaps temporarily. Most importantly, improvements in energy flow, meaning, increased food, income, social status, for example, can increase our resilience and, hopefully, help inform our decisions.

We take take our time series chart for several variables: the price of meat, the availability of meat (on a scale of 1-10), the price of fuel, and bus reliability (on a scale of 1-5).

Without doing complicated math, we will have to look carefully at the information to see what patterns we think there are.

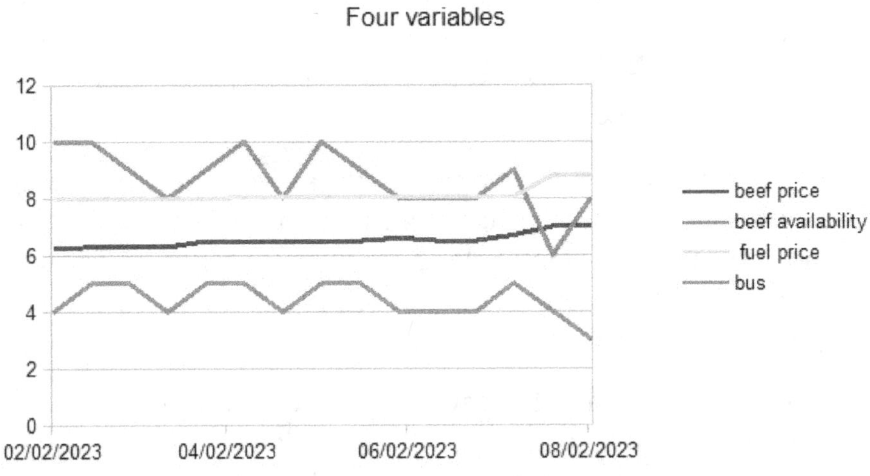

Our fictional time series chart, above, covers four variables for fifteen weeks. Four variables out of dozens we could consider doesn't seem too many, and fifteen weeks is not very long for patterns to develop.

Even so, the four variables I have chosen cover food and transportation, which will give us key information. We can think of it as taking a patient's pulse and blood pressure. We would like to have the results of many medical tests before making a diagnosis, but those two things tell us a lot about the immediate general health of the patient.

Because the time period is relatively short, and mainly covers spring, and seasonal changes can be significant, we can't guess how things will go, but we can assume that the cost of fuel might be affecting both the cost and availability of beef and the reliability of the bus system.

Clearly, though, both the cost of beef and the price of fuel have trended upward, and the availability of beef and the reliability of the bus, downward. If that continues as a trend in the long term, likely the system will significantly change.

But, we can't really guess how. Transportation might become much more expensive and less reliable, but perhaps the price of beans will come down, as producers adjust to new demand. We can't fully guess what will happen. Even so, we have trends which give us some guidance.

Because of the way we arrange our data, with, for example, the price of something changing by a hundredth (a penny), and our 1-10 quantified scale being able to change by a tenth, the measures won't have the same detail, that is, a hundredth allows more small changes than a tenth.

We can, but don't have to, determine the rate of change, or the percentage of change, expressed as a positive number when going up, and a negative when going down. We might take the rate or percentage of change in each variable, that is, the price of fuel, and so on, and compare it to the rate of change of the other variables. In our first graph, we show the full data, price and date, and in the second, we compare only the change in each group.

Do we want to do that? It would show us which variables were changing the most rapidly, and might help us correlate them in some predictive way. We can see how the rate of increase of the price of fuel and the rate of increase in the cost of beef are correlated.

By "correlated" we mean that they seem to change in some pattern together. We might guess that the price of fuel is being reflected in the price of meat, since virtually everything about raising, transporting, distributing and so on is fossil fuel dependent.

However, from our chart, we can't say that the price of fuel is causal, meaning it is the direct cause of the change, only that they are correlated, and seem to be related somehow, at some level of the system.

Later, when our information is discussed, the graph, and our understanding of networks and energy, will help us, and we might find larger system changes that explain the cause of the increase in fuel, and so the even greater increase in the cost of beef.

There are dozens of other charts and graphs, each of which is best at showing a particular kind of pattern, but our goal is to keep our methodology simple and energy efficient; we are looking for a positive energy return on energy invested. A time series is the best for our purposes, but by all means, purchase a book on statistical analysis if you have the energy.

Energy And Network Resilience In Our Analysis

What do our time series or other information studies tell us about how the system is using energy?

Our view is that the system exists because it organizes energy: physical energy, the energy of humans, and debt. The energy moves through networks.

If we look at a central street three times every day for a year, we will see changes in the flow of traffic. The traffic type might change: private cars, buses, delivery vans, trucks and tractor/trailers, bicycles, police cars, and foot traffic.

We expect the proportion of each vehicle type will change, for example from 6:00 in the morning until midnight, and a change in that pattern is informative.

This, mostly qualitative, information tells us things about the energy flowing past you on the street that we can compare to other flows to determine what the system is doing.

Prices going up and down; traffic increasing or decreasing, social unrest more or less serious, crime more or less. **Any indication of energy moving through networks is useful to us.**

5. STRATEGY AND TACTICS

Understanding How To Conclude, From Data, What Possible Actions Might Be, And What Their Likelihood Of Having A Positive Energy Return On Energy Investment Might Be

We recall mentioning the different approaches to responding to risk to the family: **buy, sell, hunker down, step forward, pay for protection, fight, or flee.**

Most situations can be addressed by one of those options, or a subtle and blended mixture of them. If we see a bargain on something which will provide surplus, and so resilience to the family, we buy it.

If we have an opportunity to unload an energy using element which is not returning sufficient energy on investment, we sell. Sometimes to get the energy to buy, we sell.

Hunker down means to withdraw into the family, often to weather some events which prevent us from energy surplus accumulation Hunker down means to avoid trading, perhaps, or to avoid community involvement, or literally, to stay in a safe place with your head low.

Stepping forward is done to gain more human energy, more status. It can mean offering your time or other energy resources to an effort, or it can mean adding your voice to others who want some kind of change, or to prevent change, in the community. Stepping forward means taking a side, which can increase your affiliation and opportunities for status, but it also acquires some competitors or, perhaps, foes.

Paying for protection is common. Citizens pay the state for protection. When society becomes less complex, we might pay a bandit king, or other source of social control for protection. It always comes at a greater cost than is obvious, since the demand for money goes up.

Even so, if the cost is low enough, and the benefit seems clear enough, using a methodology and a pragmatic, systems based approach, then we pay for protection, often just to keep the protector from beating us.

Fight means desperation. We avoid fighting all we can. We fight because we face an existential threat, and we should always expect a loss when we fight.

We avoid violence all we can. Violence often leads to more violence, which sucks our energy. Unless you are a criminal, violence usually costs more than it captures.

Before we fight, we use whatever markers of energy we can to assess our opponent. We gather data on debt energy, and that might provide an explanation for the fight from their perspective.

Always consider your opponent's perspective.

Think of all you know about the reasons people do things, about the emotions which cause them to take certain actions, and about what energy flows they have at risk. You might be able to avoid a fight, or gain an early victory, if you thoroughly understand your enemy. However, if they simply want to kill you and take what you have, fight desperately. If you are forced to fight, fight without mercy.

Even so, we never fight when we think we might lose. If we have to, and if we can, we flee.

When we flee, we still have to have some kind of plan. We also have to have agreed to some trigger event which causes us to flee, because fleeing is only better than fighting to the death if you get away. Otherwise, it is fighting an enemy behind you, which is a very poor strategy, obviously.

Fleeing under your terms, taking what you can, is a strategy but leaves you in a bad way, with few resources. Unless you have fleeing as a plan, which we discuss below.

Whatever we decide, we follow our logical system of gathering data, making information from it, and comparing it to other variables, to help us determine what might happen, and plan for it.

We recall that *"calm is a superpower."* Never more so than when preparing to do something. We need to be calm and objective while assessing the potential crisis. Even though some problems are emotionally difficult, we need to be dispassionate when we conclude what our strengths are, and where the greatest threat and/or benefit lies.

First, we discuss what we think the problem is, and **then we speculate on what the cause might be.**

In many instances, as we discuss what the problem is, we often change our initial assessment. As the discussion reaches farther from the identified problem, we see the important underlying issues, the networks of all kinds and changes there.

It is thorny, because immediacy always takes priority. Likely, we should look at the underlying causes and take action to prepare or offset those, but we have to instead, act to deal with the issue at hand.

In other words, if a drunk driver crosses the center line and weaves into your lane, it does little good to know that he is drunk, and that alcohol is a major source of car accidents, you just need to jump left or jump right.

It is for this reason, though, that we do all this work, so that we reduce the seriousness of sudden crisis by expecting it early.

If we watch the drunk driver far enough ahead, we can slow, and expect to need to suddenly brake and perhaps leave the road. (Incidentally, people often realize they have left their lane and swerve back into it; slowing and trying to pull off the road gives your greatest likelihood of avoiding an accident.)

We want to use our predictive power to see as far ahead as possible, keeping in mind that something else might happen as the crisis approaches. We cannot know for certain. This is true of everything, small and immediate and massive and far off.

However, our near estimations are more likely to be accurate than our distant ones, because there are fewer events, fewer changes in variables. This is not magic; it is educated guesswork. So, we start our discussion with something small and near.

For Example, The Bus!

We have already discussed things that can make the bus late, or unreliable. They include things like the cost of fuel, rider patterns, and many other things.

Most of those, in a functional social system, would be temporary problems, usually solved with more energy (so, the fare goes up).

Let's break our issue down.

The problem:

We use the bus to go to work and to shop. When it is on time, it is relatively cheap and energy efficient for us. We can use our time efficiently.

If the bus is not reliable, that is a problem for us. We might not get our groceries home, or we might lose our job for being late, or be late to pick up our child from school, leading to a social services call.

There are alternatives:

Determine the amount of energy you save over each alternative, below, by determining a starting value of using the bus, quantify the costs of using the bus in fare and time, to establish a base line.

However, create three levels, one with perfect timeliness and fare, one which is unreliable by half an hour, and one where the bus never came, or came but was full and you missed getting a seat, increasing your stay half an hour or more. If you like, you can increase each by a potential fee increase.

Those estimations will form the basis of seeking an alternative. And to determining how much energy, in terms of money and time, each will take from your energy total.

What alternatives do we have, and what do they cost, in terms of money and time.

In making educated guesses at some values, or quantifying qualities, the information we need most is available if we use three levels, or more, if the situation requires it, of severity, or benefit in the predictions we seek. Using three levels of loss allows you to do a meaningful cost benefit analysis.

We note here, and will do so again, that a decline involves a reduction in energy, which means cops and firefighters and EMTs and road crews are less available. This presents higher risk, from crime, but also because bad roads are hard on cars, and blocked city arteries means driving much further to reach your destination, and so on.

Noting this, we weight our estimations in every instance, such that, at some point, it might become too dangerous to walk, for example, but fuel costs might be high, increasing the cost of all travel.

Societal collapse means constantly expecting things to get worse, and being able to adapt to the new circumstances.

These are common options, but you might find other options which satisfy your family's needs.

Own a car, if we have the resources to afford one:

Advantage: always available and reliable, time efficient. Depending on your own needs, quantify those energy advantages.

Cost: because of insurance and registration, a car costs you when you aren't using it. It uses space or costs money to store. It uses fuel. It breaks down, needs tires, or could be stolen. It could be in an accident, and if it is your fault, you might be sued. The highest per mile cost if only driven a small amount, because of fixed costs.

Make a guess at the likelihood of each potential cost and aggregate three levels.

We can do this by both likelihood and cost. The base, meaning, low level cost, includes things that there are a 100% or at least a very high percentage certainty of cost: actual cost of insurance, license and storage; a determination of how frequently it would need tires.

A second, higher level of cost would include breakdowns and small accidents. Those have a high cost, and a moderate likelihood, because anyone who drives very much eventually has a fender bender or a serious mechanical problem.

The most serious costs are theft, carjacking, and injury or fatality accidents; the cost on those are very high, but the likelihood is relatively low, **depending**, again, on the state of the system generally.

Taxi, essentially a car you own for a very limited period:

Advantage: usually available; more time efficient than the bus; limited liability;

Cost: much more expensive than the bus per mile, and comparable to a frequently driven car. Long distances diminish the advantage over owning a car. In addition, a new one is needed for every stop, and they cost money while they wait.

Here, we can find some useful variables to discuss. Are the resources there to afford a taxi? Are most trips to town just one stop, or many? How far will the trip be? Do taxis save us enough time that it offsets the cost over the bus? Can we recapture some of the costs by doing shopping for others as a business?

You know your family's strengths, and can improve on these few alternatives.

Ride share, neighborhood ride co-ops, other informal transportation systems:

Advantage: cheaper than the taxi. No upkeep or storage costs.

Disadvantage: these tend to work only certain hours, are not on a hard timetable, have crowding if they get full.

Bicycle:

Advantage: probably the best investment per mile. With a bike trailer and saddle baskets, can take a significant load, perhaps more than by bus. There are at least a billion bicycles in the world, and perhaps more. It is how poor people around the world travel if they can.

Disadvantage: slower than motorized travel; less protection in extreme heat, or other harsh weather; less protection from theft or robbery; requires a great deal of human energy (it's ok to get off and push it for awhile!).

Walk:

This is how people have traveled throughout most of our history.

Advantage: the cheapest per mile.

Disadvantage: slow. Limited cargo capacity. No protection from weather or thugs.

As you go through the alternatives, you might simply give each a general score, and compare that. That is a starting place to discuss and decision make. Or, you could go a little farther and specify, resolving, for example, that:

If it is a daytime trip of less than ten miles with limited need for cargo on public streets, the bicycle is better than the expensive and unreliable bus. Bring a bike lock.

If weather is bad or it is dark, or the route is dangerous, check to see if a neighborhood transport will go in your direction at a schedule that works for you. If the issues are bad weather and darkness, expect a higher demand, so it might not be easy to get one. If you don't have to go, stay home.

If the distance round trip is great, or it is foul weather, dangerous location, or darkness, take a taxi. Otherwise, stay home.

If the trip is frequent, long, with large cargoes or several passengers, get a car if you can.

Consider moving, changing jobs, grocery delivery or other ways to avoid travel.

As always, when you do your planning, expect things to get worse.

Being Used To Bad News

But, how worse? When?

As we have discussed, on the one hand, we can't know, but on the other hand, we can detect when a network is losing energy. The bus doesn't go out as far as it did. It costs more and more to take the bus. Criminals ride the bus. The bus is unreliable.

If we see these things coming, we have a heads up. If we need our job and current lifestyle, we get a car and eat gruel to feed the car gas, and so on. The car will perhaps become sufficiently useful that you can risk your life to be a taxi driver. That might be a way to profit while the system declines: put energy into getting and safely storing a car and take calls to give rides for cash. (Strangers sit behind you all day and night.)

To do that wisely, you have to determine how long gas will be readily available, how long the streets will be safe enough to travel; it could be years.

To pause to put things into focus, the conditions we describe as miserable from the perspective of a middle or lower class of citizen in the West have been every day life for an innumerable number of people on a good day across the world. Most people in the US will have water and sewer for a long time, whereas, as I write this, at least 2 billion people globally lack a source of clean water nearby.

In those places, people find ways to live. Hygiene there is difficult, and so disease is more prominent. Transportation in many places is crowded now, taking cargo is difficult, breakdowns are common, but they make things work. If a bus breaks down, an empty truck going the same way will take paying passengers, for example.

We should be stalwart enough to live as the poorest of the world have lived. Find ways to make do. Time is mostly what is lost in those transportation systems.

And, speaking of time, when? When will we in our home live like the poor of the rest of the world? As we know, we cannot know, but we can watch and try to plan.

Using our same method of creating information from data, and using trends in simple charts, we can ask more difficult questions.

A good start might be to discuss something with not much math, but a lot of gathering of information and deep consideration:

Should We Buy A Firearm?

There are reasons to have a firearm. In violent times, a firearm won't protect you, but it will even the odds in some instances. As evidence of the importance of firearms, we pause to consider that thieves try to steal them, and so does the government.

However, there is much to consider.

A firearm delivers force over a distance. All it takes to kill a human are strong hands, or a solid stick two inches in diameter and two feet long. There are many weapons in every household, from hammers to frying pans, but the firearm allows for distance from the threat, and a reliable destructive blow.

Should we buy a firearm:

Is it dangerous to go out on the street?

Gathering data from all sources, how likely are we to be involved in crime?

Does law enforcement do a good job of keeping the streets safe?

Is there a trend, either general impression or in our data, that indicates crime might get worse?

Can some of us shoot someone? Are there family members willing to use deadly force in an emergency?

The family does research on those issues. Who thinks they could shoot someone if the family or themselves were at risk of violence?

How much will one cost?

How much will ammunition cost?

What are the laws where we live regarding firearms ownership?

Will it increase or negate family insurance?

And, whatever other questions that arise with your research.

What are the disadvantages of firearms ownership?

Here are some fast facts:

If you use your firearm improperly, and plant a slug in some innocent person, you will have massive legal bills and perhaps go to prison, and might have preferred to simply have been beaten a little and robbed.

It is possible that if you have a firearm you might be more likely to be shot as a threat, whereas without it, you might be allowed to live as a victim.

You are more likely to die from a firearm if you have one in the house. However, we should critically consider what that means.

 In most years, about half of firearms deaths are suicide. We can assume that the person decided to end their lives in what they hoped was a painless manner (warning! This is not always the case!), and might instead have chosen pills or auto-strangulation.

Many people who live or work in crime ridden areas carry a firearm, but might be killed with a firearm. Gang members often have firearms, and are sometimes killed with firearms.

However, if you have someone in the house who is addicted to alcohol, or pills or other hard drugs, they will be a potential liability the family should consider.

It is possible people will try to kill you to get your firearm. This is because, in violent situations, a firearm can be lifesaving. People will kill with a rock to get the advantage of a firearm.

What kind of firearm should we get:

Your family does research and learns something along the lines of this: If you are considering getting a firearm, it is only sensible to go to a gun shop, preferably one with an indoor or outdoor range, and to take firearms safety courses. Firearms are dangerous, and are safe only when properly handled.

To speed our discussion, I offer this quick assessment, which is just an example. It is not intended to be complete, and experts might disagree with parts, and so on, so do your own research, this is just a starter:

There are categories of firearms, both in use and in the law.

Primer type:

In general, there are two primer types. Rimfire and centerfire. Rimfire now comes only in .22 long rifle, two forms of .22 magnum, and a .17 round. The most commonly found is the .22 lr.

The .22 lr is a small bullet of, usually, between 30 and 40 grains. It is not heavy, does not go fast (velocity depends on load and barrel length). While not very powerful, in the hands of a skilled shooter, it can kill anything from a mouse to a moose, and certainly humans.

However, to do that, shot placement is everything. Few people can shoot that well, especially under stress. Many people and animals die from .22 injuries, but sometimes not when you need them to. Larger calibers have more "stopping power", meaning the target is incapacitated more quickly. Rimfire semiautomatics are more likely to misfire or hang up, since the forces are relatively small.

Advantage: the .22 is the most useful firearm to have, since rounds are cheap and easy to carry. They cannot be reloaded.

Centerfire. This employs a separate primer in the center of the round. Rounds are available in centerfire from .17 to .50 calibers.

Advantage: power, function in the firearm, and some common types can be reloaded.

Handguns

Handguns come in many calibers, from .22 lr to .50 Smith and Wesson. Still handguns have less power than many rifles.

Handguns are difficult to shoot well. If your family decided to get a handgun, you need to practice often. Useful range for a handgun is honestly from the muzzle (point blank) to 50 yards. Past that, it becomes difficult to hit the target reliably.

Handguns are easy to conceal, one real virtue.

Action types range from single action revolver, where the hammer must be drawn back each time, to double action revolvers, where pulling the trigger turns the cylinder and fires the shot, to the semiautomatic pistol.

Single action revolver is better than nothing, but shots are far between, since it has to be cocked every time.

Double action revolver is the most reliable; if a cylinder doesn't fire, you pull the trigger again and a new round is under the hammer. Jams can happen, but they are rare. Most hold from 10 rounds for .22lr to five or six rounds, with six being the most common. After six rounds, you must reload.

Semiautomatic pistols are generally in calibers from .22lr to .44 magnum, with 9mm being the most common. They can fire up to 16 rounds before inserting a new magazine. Magazines are usually quicker to change than reloading a revolver. Larger calibers have considerable recoil, especially in lighter firearms.

Semiautomatics of all kinds jam more than other actions.

Some feel the 9mm is marginal for stopping power, but it is easy to shoot, the ammunition is widely available, and it is used by police and military around the world. There are even carbines and short rifles chambered for it.

Long guns

Long guns are the easiest to shoot and most powerful. An average shooter can hit a human sized target from the barrel to 100 yards. Many rifles are lethal to over 2000 yards.

Rifle barrels most commonly range from about 16 to 28 inches, but some are longer. A long gun with a short barrel (usually 16-20 inches) is a "carbine." Rifle calibers range from .22 lr to .50 Browning Machine Gun.

Actions include bolt action in either single shot or repeater (holds rounds in a magazine for the next shot), lever action, pump, and semi-auto or auto (currently, few people have a permit for fully auto; they also eat a huge amount of ammunition, and most shots miss).

Shotguns are also long guns. The most common sized shotguns are 12 gauge, 20 gauge, and .410, in decreasing order of barrel size. The .410 is somewhat marginal for defense. The 12 gauge is the most popular, but has considerable recoil. Many people consider a 20 gauge to be more than adequate.

Shotguns come in single shot, double barrel, pump, and semiautomatic actions, though there are a few bolt and lever shotguns.

A shot gun is a short range weapon, but very effective in its range. It can fire small shot, which are dangerous up to about 30 yards, or buckshot, which fires several round balls and are dangerous to 75 yards (but might easily miss at that range), and the solid slug, which is deadly out to 100 yards, or more in the hands of a skilled shooter.

Long guns are more difficult to move around in tight areas, and easier to take away in close quarters.

Popular semiautomatic long guns are the AR-15 (the title is misapplied to many similar modern ergonomic weapons) in the most popular cartridge of 5.56mm; and the Iron Curtain favorite, the AK-47 (likewise a name used for similar firearms) in 7.62x39. Currently, ammunition in both calibers are available in bulk, since both are military rounds. Most 7.62x39 are not easily reloadable. (Obviously, research "reloading".)

That is just a short list of things to consider; if your family is considering getting a firearm, get one from a reputable shop, and members should take classes in safety, firing drills, and strategies. If you have the energy.

Losing a family member to a household firearm is emotionally devastating. Ceaselessly practice safety.

After discussion, and considering all risks and costs, does the family need a firearm?

If there were people kicking in our front door, would we need a firearm? Do we need more than one?

Do we need something else, like pepper spray?

Now, a more difficult example.

Should We Stay Where We Are, Or Should We Move?

This is a significant question. Earlier we mentioned in passing that essential strategies were to buy, sell, hunker down, step forward, pay for protection, fight, or flee. Leaving our current location and moving to a more favorable one is a massive question.

First of all, because the idea of "more favorable" is relative, both to your personal skills and economic energy, and to "when." It depends how far in the future you plan for. Again, we recall, decline and collapse means becoming accustomed to bad news.

The idea of leaving the city and moving to a sustainable place in a tight community in the hills is not new. People have been making that move for at least the last 70 years. Many people have moved, some to farms outside the city that eventually became suburbs; others moved far from any community, into the woods, into the swamp, into the mountains. They mostly don't want you to come there, why would they?

Likewise, the idea of "living off the land" has many problems. First, the land is changing, and soon weather will no longer be seasonally predictable. In addition, people going back to the land to survive have taken a toll on the environment. Farming is often difficult for the best farmers in the best of times.

People leaving one environment and surviving several years in another have a high failure rate, just as people who leave the country to go to the city to start a business do. Changing your environment is difficult.

One reason for leaving the city is the fear of being trapped there when food becomes short. However, cities are the nexus of the system, they will have food when the countryside is hungry. Cities and governments have often simply gone to the farms and taken their produce, often dictating what they should grow.

There may be reasons for leaving the city during a decline or collapse. Some people will actually continue to thrive better in the city.

And, that is a key question your family has to ask: can you rapidly adapt to a completely new environment, leaving or going to the city or country.

Moving takes time and energy, getting established in some persistent manner requires time to understand the local markets, the alliances people form locally, the amount of surplus energy in the community, by which we mean, cheap electricity, or a ready and skilled workforce hungry for a job, the level of life most local people have. Remember, familiarity, similarity and proximity? How are those social networks of people organized to accept you, or keep you out?

Many people think of moving to a suburban or slightly distant peripheral place. Here there might be some reasonable compromise, not close enough for the crime of the city, but near enough to access resources.

If you have the economic energy to do that, and live there sustainably, that might be a consideration. Many families won't. Likely, it will be a temporary solution. Every choice you make will be a temporary solution; those are the solutions we have in decline.

So, the discussion has touched on some key data points and we need to seek that data.

If you have considered moving, you have no doubt already thought of all these things, since they are essential to leaving one energy stream and moving into another.

You have to try to determine the cost-benefit of each decision, and on key decisions, you want to test it out with "what if it happens, what if it doesn't." We always need to consider that, because that gives us our range. If it doesn't happen or if it does, implies a level of risk. If the difference between the two is negligible, or if you have a sound secondary strategy because you asked the question, the risk is less.

So, this is not a complete list, just a start:

Energy resources

Current debt energy, including:

Actual debt, your credit stance: do you owe money, or do you have a large credit resource?

Money in savings, checking, and disposable bonds and stocks

Cash on hand

Salable unneeded items

A car

A house

Rental property

A business

A profession or skill which is marketable everywhere

If your assets are the basis of your income, you can't count them as debt energy unless you can replace them in your income.

Time: what timeline do you have?

Is the market for your house shrinking and the market for rural property, or vice versa, sinking?

If there will be gap between income sources, when is the best time to move to minimize that gap?

Is decline happening too rapidly?

If you wait, will you be too old?

Do you have a certification or other documentation that expires?

Energy over time is always critical. Ideally, you would make a smooth transition, meaning you would lose little of the three kinds of energy.

Social assets

Family in the new location

A denomination with a church there

Children under 16; children more rapidly integrate a family in a community

A job in the new area

Membership in a club or organization with a presence in the new community

Associated energy costs

The cost of moving

The human physical energy of moving

The social risk of moving

Whether, after sale of disposable items like houses and other items is completed, you have enough money to buy or rent something in the new place

Deposits for new utilities

Any repairs your old place needs or the new place requires before the transition

Since you know your family's situation, you will find other questions to ask, meaning things to gather data for, and then turn that data into information.

We have to do the hard work, break things out and put them down in an organized fashion, and come up with three or so alternatives, each of which is implied or suggested by our work, and we discuss and weigh between them.

Quick examples; after discussing and weighing our sense of the flows of energy, we come up with:

1. Don't move at all. Turn paper assets into equity in what you have. Buy other neighboring houses when the market is soft (assuming you have been doing a time study and know its behavior) and improve them, or turn one into a business.

2. Sell everything and move across town. Though prices are very high there, we can crowd the family into an apartment and all get jobs, establish business networks in the neighborhood, at some point, turn the new savings and equity into a larger or more secure place.

3. Sell everything and go back to great grandma's home town. Because of fuel costs, people are leaving it to be closer to the city, and your dollar will buy more. Get a place with water rights and pasture and woods just out of town, or buy a small business. Introduce your kids to the school, or pick a large congregation and become devout; make sure someone goes to service every week. Pay attention to how people dress, and who is related to whom. Have the entire family work their hands into callouses in the business, or the farm, or both.

Likely none of these will fit your family, and they are just an example of three options we might resolve to consider.

Whatever you do, have a clear understanding of what the location has, that you are leaving, what the energy flows will be like there as time goes by.

It may even be that the family separates, at least for awhile. However, when thinking of delinking family, always consider what we know of humans, how context driven they are, and how important similarity, familiarity and especially proximity are.

Plan B

Ideally, we would have plenty of debt energy, which would buy us status and make everything easy. However, that is unlikely, in part because we always want to do better than we easily can. Surplus energy accrues very slowly, typically, to families who just tread water. You often have to have some risk when you want to accrue energy faster. Hence, however much we have, it is reasonable to try to risk to that point.

But, having done our "what if it does, what if it doesn't" homework through the entire process, we have ideas of where failure might occur.

In the example of moving, above, our most dangerous case comes when we sell our stuff, and are moving to the new place. Many things can go wrong which would strand us between the two.

That is a difficult place to work from, and requires expensive accommodations which drain our resources and so future success. If we leave our networks without energy for too long, the return is very difficult.

For this reason, **at every important juncture of our process of moving or making a major change, we should have a second plan to fall back on.**

This plan should help minimize energy loss, and should even

have at least a rough ledger: if something falls through at the last minute with our first choice, we try to smoothly transition to our second choice.   That is, make an offer on something else and camp out.

If you have sunk costs, like a rented van full of your stuff, you are left to decide on temporary storage, or the continued rental, but not actual use of, the van. Or, a similar problem if you have a mover store your goods.

It might be a plan to rent in the area and not buy right away.

The problem with Plan B is that it often takes energy to prepare, and that energy is frozen or lost if nothing goes wrong.

Plan B is insurance against total loss, and like any insurance you are betting against yourself. If you have a sufficient number of Plans B, you might not have energy left to accomplish your main goal.

Or, worse, your excellent alternative plans might short your main effort enough that it almost, but not quite, succeeds. In many instances, "almost but not quite" is the worst case. You have spent all you have and have fallen short of your goal, and are perhaps left in a kind of costly limbo. Leap from one tree to another and almost, but not quite, make it.

So, each Plan B will have to follow the same methodology as the original question, including "what if this thing happens, what do we lose, what if it doesn't, what have we lost by preparing for it."

We can't predict every event, or how serious every event is. People who are more likely to survive are those who can "read the winds" of coming change, make thoughtful, informed decisions, and take actions. People doing that throughout our history are why we are here.

6. LET'S USE WHAT WE HAVE LEARNED AND PREDICT THE COLLAPSE OF COMPLEX GLOBAL SOCIETY!

First, we have learned that we cannot predict the collapse of global society! But, it sure would be nice to know, and we can watch for signs the system is beginning to lose networks, starting to lose energy and to use what energy it has less efficiently.

We have learned that the system lives on energy and does not "choose" to "do this," but rather, like a river, finds its way around the obstacles in the environment, following energy, changing them as it does so.

The system survives by, essentially, organizing three kinds of energy, physical energy, like things that burn; and human energy, as humans busily recreate the system over and over from instant to instant, each following their own propensities in the context as they understand it; and debt energy, which is a kind of human energy which allows value and exchange to take place over long distances, and literally permeate the globe, with networks effecting nearly all humans on the planet.

We have learned that humans will be human; they will react to the world according to their propensities, in a context created by the system, always being aware of status, and will have "differential association," meaning they will be generous to some but not others. Humans are hierarchical, and incredibly social.

We have learned that collapse is usually not uniform in the way that it descends. Like an injured or dying animal, the system will constantly reallocate energy towards the core. However, we have learned that it can drop suddenly, with all networks failing, like a sudden heart attack.

We have learned that collapse is global, but we have to act with immediacy, meaning the needs of living and the struggle to accumulate energy. We have also learned that a system can collapse when it seems to be doing well, but interior stresses and failures make it fragile.

We have learned that the system operates on, and is given "shape" by, networks. Some networks are short, and see most of their activity on foot; some are many thousands of miles long, touching land, sea, and air.

Networks most often use physical energy to move human and debt energy, but some networks exist only in the way individual humans interact. We know we can measure and track the three kinds of energy to get some understanding of the resilience of the networks we rely on for life.

We have learned that weather makes history, because it effects energy. Though our species is 300,000 years old, it is only since the end of the last "ice age" when the climate became unusually warm and stable, that our numbers rapidly grew.

As the weather becomes hotter and more unstable, the system will collapse, and people will die by the millions, from exposure, and thirst, and hunger, and violence. We cannot predict the weather, but we can understand the essentials and consequences of climate.

We have learned that the planet is very badly overpopulated at 8 billion people, and it is projected to grow by two more billion (but probably won't). We know that the system of culture organized energy to produce this huge population. That human energy, as the system collapses, will be disorganized, for a little while, before the population drops.

How soon, how bad? (Or, how bad, how soon?)

I will proceed, first, by outlining, at this writing, what **I think the possible perturbations to the energy parameters of the global social system are**. In our immediate world, it will mean, fast or slow, a general decline in the reliability of the necessities of life.

1. Climate Change/Pollution, Environmental Destruction

The weather is going to get worse. It will get hotter, or wetter, or windier, but most of all, it will be unpredictable. If it were just getting hotter, we could all scooch north or south a bit.

For example, this summer, 2023, was, by far, the hottest across the globe. Winter in the Southern Hemisphere was mostly too warm, and in the North, there were blazing hot days, with Turkey, for example, experiencing a searing 50C/122F. Since there has been a steady increase in the generalized highs for more than a decade, some experts believe we will not likely see a cooler summer.

The dramatic increases in temperature and CO2 saturation mean the seas will change, and are changing, as they reach the limits of the heat they can absorb. A hot, acid sea does not feed people. Some areas of the sea continue to produce large amounts of food, but in most places on the globe, harvests from the sea are also becoming less certain.

Separate issues are the general, and perhaps unstoppable, decline in species on land and in the seas, and pollution by literally every chemical or isotope we have produced.

The impact of climate change and the loss of arable land and fresh water on food production will be significant.

A quick rundown of a few of those who recognize the climate is rapidly changing, and what they think can be done.

If you are curious, do your own research; I present these as part of our methodology exercise, and they are incomplete, and omit other important perspectives. However, most of them look for a target planetary heat of 1.5 C above 1880, though it seems inevitable at this point it will go higher. Here are some predictions and suggested remedies:

IPCC Intergovernmental Panel on Climate Change, from the United Nations.

The essence of the IPCC approach is that we have to work to reduce damage to the environment, and end inequality notably between the West and the rest of the Global South, to reduce resource use among the richest nations, to reduce the distance from food, and so on. The group predicts that, if we do nothing, life will get harder and the chances of avoiding catastrophe will diminish if we don't make major changes now. It will be hell on earth by 2100-2400. In the most recent report, they call for 1.5C[7] before 2050.

The IPCC projections[8] have consistently proven to underestimate the rapidity with which change is coming. It is a product of a global perspective on action, with science that has been sifted by politicians, and seems, to me, to be unlikely to change anything significantly.

In my view the IPCC fails to fully understand and accommodate issues of the system itself; the panel focuses on human agency, action, and believes, because that is what we believe today, that humans control the system; this is uninformed. It is a system; it runs on energy, and actually requires inequality, for example, so surplus can be gathered.

There is really no solid evidence that we can sufficiently reduce the quality of life of the West to have sufficient energy to protect the environment and support a huge human population at any level of existence. Regardless the science of their own report, the panel continues to talk about "sustainable development". The goal is to get as many people as possible, and still save the environment.

The Club of Rome

In the 1960s a discussion led to an informal group of scientists of various sorts and businessmen, mostly of the wealthy sort. The history says they concluded, essentially, that the approach to growth and resource use, and other problems we have discussed, was unsustainable. It was proposed that only a comprehensive approach could avoid serious social disaster.

In 1972, in *Limits to Growth*[9], the authors used an early computer program to plot out the depletion of certain metals, if use trends continued. It assumed the growth rate of use, or, to look at it the other way around, the continued growing rate of depletion, would lead to a sudden societal collapse "in the next 100 years." It has been over 50 years since that prediction.

There have been many other models since, and they take climate change and energy depletion into account. That prediction has not changed too much.

The LTG review left the realm of science and entered that of social science. They insisted it would be possible to give everyone on the planet a good life, and still preserve the environment.

In 1972 there were 3.8 billion people. There are now twice that many, nearly 8 billion. There are debates about how many people have actually had their lives improved, relative to the depletion of not only mineral resources, but the environment in general, and, we add, climate change.

Guy McPherson

McPherson, is a professor of natural resources, ecology and evolutionary biology at University of Arizona. He has been called a "doom cult leader" who has built a reputation for feeding the worst possible news to the gullible.

Around 2007, he made a number of predictions, none of which have yet come true, including the inevitability of near term human extinction. People with all kinds of interests denigrated McPherson as a know-nothing about climate change or human technology.

In 2018 he predicted there would be no humans left alive by 2026, due, he said, to projections for climate change and because of the collapse of so many species on which we rely.

My take on McPherson is that he does a good job of looking at our situation and discussing the connectedness of the complex system of networks which keep us alive. He has said most people would die from starvation, depredation and suicide; many die of starvation, depredation and suicide now.

His dire prediction requires an extremely abrupt collapse. I think the system is too big, there are too many resources in cities for such an abrupt end; however it is certainly possible.

McPherson considers nearly every variable, including poorly maintained nuclear plants poisoning lakes, rivers and seas. While the far more socially acceptable scientists at CoR and IPCC feel we can somehow correct our crisis with social remedies, more pragmatic McPherson suggests, even if that were all possible, there isn't time.

In my view, he had pegged the "how bad," but not the "how soon," meaning his view is compressed. Today (September 4, 2023) I heard him say, in an interview, that we have just a few years left, at most, before the climate hits so many tipping points it will no doubt flip this year or next, and start killing people everywhere.

If that is the case, you will never see this book. However, stretch it out just a little, a few decades, and it is falling in line with other predictions of collapse, including LTG.

McPherson's remedy for impending collapse? "Live a life of excellence."

However bad it might become some day, we need to know how to make decisions to live today. Our ancestors lived in spite of sometimes terrifying odds, and here we are. Let's see what we can do.

Using those timelines and perspectives, they represent a collapse event spread of from now (as I write this), to about the turn of the century.

But precisely when will the end be, and what will it be like? If I knew that I would have mentioned it much earlier in the book. However, I will gather data, consider energy flows, and make an informed guess, for the purposes of example, and the fun of doing this kind of wild and crazy prediction.

2. Economy/Energy

I have rolled two energies into one: debt energy and physical energy.

As we have noted, debt energy is the hybrid of human energy and physical energy. Debt energy is real because people act as if it were real. Without that, currency and digital fortunes would not have any value.

On the other hand, though, **the economy is inexorably associated with physical energy**. Without it, resources stay in the ground, people and trade goods travel by foot.

To be clear, for a few thousand years complex societies functioned on grass: grains for humans and fodder for livestock and wild game. With just these meager sources of energy, cities and tribal societies managed to kill and conquer, and take slaves.

However, a global society powered by grass could not have supported eight billion, or any billion people. Wind powered ships facilitated killing, slaving, and trade in general.

That actually, historically, brings us to the age of coal, beginning, about the late 1700s. Humans had been using coal for, perhaps, tens of thousands of years, but only incidentally, About 4,000 BC people actively mined coal and built industries on it.

However, it was the European Industrial Revolution that made coal indispensable. That is also when our pollution of the sky with carbon began.

We think of the story of Singapore, and the photos of Houston and Tokyo at night. Those networks run on energy. As physical energy declines, debt energy will decline, and as it declines, many networks will reorganize locally at a lower level of complexity, or disappear.

We should predict ghost towns everywhere, and scavengers creating new, shorter networks with the residual energy of the past nexus; some day, but when?

For today, the International Monetary Fund update for 2023 says:

"Global growth is projected to fall from an estimated 3.5 percent in 2022 to 3.0 percent in both 2023 and 2024. While the forecast for 2023 is modestly higher than predicted in the April 2023 World Economic Outlook (WEO), it remains weak by historical standards. The rise in central bank policy rates to fight inflation continues

to weigh on economic activity. Global headline inflation is expected to fall from 8.7 percent in 2022 to 6.8 percent in 2023 and 5.2 percent in 2024. Underlying (core) inflation is projected to decline more gradually, and forecasts for inflation in 2024 have been revised upward."[10]

We pause here to recall that the Gross Domestic Product, or whatever measure is used, must show growth. No economy can have no growth for very long; the system requires surplus energy, or growth.

Looking into the current state of the global system, we see a report from the World Bank:

"Global growth is projected to slow significantly amid high inflation, tight monetary policy, and more restrictive credit conditions. The possibility of more widespread bank turmoil and tighter monetary policy could result in even weaker global growth and lead to financial dislocations in the most vulnerable emerging market and developing economies (EMDEs). Comprehensive policy action is needed to foster macroeconomic and financial stability. Among many EMDEs, and especially in low-income countries, bolstering fiscal sustainability will require generating higher revenues, making spending more efficient, and improving debt management practices"[11]

The price of energy is a measure of two things: the value of the energy and the value of your currency. If the value of oil in some other measure stays the same, but your dollar is worth less, that is a reflection of inflation in your country.

However, if there is less energy, and if it takes more energy to get less energy back, (remember, energy return on energy investment) as when fracking wells deliver less overall energy for the energy it took to blast hot chemicals into the earth, than older wells did.

Statista Research says,

"Like all commodities, energy prices are largely governed by the relationship between product supply and demand. Furthermore, market speculation and geopolitical events are main drivers behind price development. This was the case in 2022 when the Russia-Ukraine war and resulting sanctions on Russia further exacerbated an ongoing global fuel shortage, leading to a 100 point rise in the fuel energy price index between August 2021 and March 2022. Meanwhile, the 2022 annual weighted price index of energy is expected to grow by nearly 50 points compared to the previous year.[12]"

An indicator of scarcity is an increase in price. The quote mentions an "ongoing global fuel shortage."

At this writing, diesel prices continue to increase, effecting the price of energy. There is still no way to replace diesel for transportation, and there will likely never be.

How far from "healthy" is the oil economy? From an IMF working paper[13]:

"This paper provides a comprehensive global, regional, and country-level update of: (i) efficient fossil fuel prices to reflect supply and environmental costs; and (ii) subsidies implied by charging below efficient fuel prices. Globally, fossil fuel subsidies were $7 trillion in 2022 or 7.1 percent of GDP. Explicit subsidies (undercharging for supply costs) have more than doubled since 2020 but are still only 18 percent of the total subsidy, while nearly 60 percent is due to undercharging for global warming and local air pollution. Differences between efficient prices and retail fuel prices are large and pervasive, for example, 80 percent of global coal consumption was priced at below half of its efficient level in 2022. Full fossil fuel price reform would reduce global carbon dioxide emissions to an estimated 43 percent below baseline levels in 2030 (in line with keeping global warming to 1.5-2oC), while raising revenues worth 3.6 percent of global GDP and preventing 1.6 million local air pollution deaths per year. Accompanying spreadsheets provide detailed results for 170

countries."

Note, the report says that, at this time, governments subsidize fossil fuel prices. Let's guess that is because **it is getting more expensive to pump and deliver fossil fuel products, and the economies might collapse if people had to pay the "efficient," or actual, cost**.

Gail Tverberg, a gifted statistician, recently made this remark in a report on stagnated fossil fuel exports:

"The indications of Figure 8 show that apart from Canada, the amount of oil exported for all the other export groupings shown is lower in recent years than it was a few years ago. This is also evident in Figure 7, but not as clearly.

"To some extent, the lower production in recent years is related to the cutbacks announced by OPEC+ (including what I call Russia+). While these cutbacks are "voluntary," they reflect the fact that based on current oil prices, and based on investments made in recent years, these countries have made the decision to cut back production. No oil exporter would dare mention that it is running short of oil that can be extracted without considerably more investment"[14].

Not fully convincing, but sufficient for our example here.

In my research on the issue, I find there is a shift in the discussion of "peak oil," meaning the point at which oil abundance begins to decline, to one of "peak demand." It doesn't matter if oil and gas production decline, because we are going to transition to green energy.

But, green energy requires fossil fuels, lots of it. A large share of oil energy goes to transportation. Making transportation "green" means going to electricity. At this writing, many grids already restrict when electric vehicles can be charged, and there is growing concern that the grid in many places can't support the increase of going to electric cars.

Natural gas and coal account for 60% of electricity. There is always an energy loss when converting from one kind to another. Electricity requires batteries, which are heavy and expensive, with constituents which require fossil fuels to mine, process, transport and so on.

While experts disagree, I side with those who believe it will never be possible to run our current system on anything except greenhouse gas producing fossil fuels, and those are rapidly running out.

3. Social Unrest

At this writing, there are 24 protests active within nations. They include political actions against some or another action by their governments. Currently, every major nation has protests and civil unrest.

According to an article in Global News[15], "austerity," or a reduction in living standard, is often the cause of protest. In France this year (2023) a change in the age of retirement caused days long protests, with violence and Molotov Cocktails to underscore the seriousness.

A report from the Center for Strategic and International Studies says, "We are living in an age of global mass protests that are historically unprecedented in frequency, scope, and size." The executive summary says:

"Mass protests increased annually by an average of 11.5 percent from 2009 to 2019 across all regions of the world, with the largest concentration of activity in the Middle East and North Africa and the fastest rate of growth in sub-Saharan Africa.

Analysis of the underlying drivers of this growth suggests the trend will continue, meaning the number and intensity of global protests is likely to increase.

Protests have resulted in a broad range of outcomes, ranging from regime change and political accommodation to protracted political violence with many casualties.

Factors that could increase the rate of protest include slowing global economic growth, worsening effects of climate change, and foreign meddling in internal politics via disinformation and other tactics."[16]

 In Analysis of World Protests, 2006-2020, the authors state:

"Our analysis of 2809 events reflects an increasing number of protests from 2006 to 2020. *Protests occur in all world regions and across all country income levels. The study found a greater prevalence of protests in middle-income countries (1327 events) and high-income countries (1122 protests) than in low-income countries (121 events).There are also a number of international and global protests that happened in multiple countries simultaneously, and their number also keeps increasing steadily over the years (239 protests)*[17]*."*

Protests do not mean collapse. Sometimes protests fail, or have harsh backlash. Most often, they simply indicate a loss of surplus for selected groups, or a strata of society. Still, protests are often part of collapse, both because it is a measure of societal decline, but also because it disrupts the social flow.

Trust declines, and people stop believing in the context of the system, and in the social world, as we know, things are only real if people perceive them as real.

Just as some systems theorists see war as relieving stress and reallocating energy, some see waves of protest as quasi-periodic but repeating in society, for those same reasons.

From a strictly theoretical perspective, the different protests display areas of stress, and though most protests change little, eventually one will provide a new direction for the system to focus energy. That doesn't mean much to us here, though!

4. Migration

We can view migration as an indicator of social unrest. **People usually migrate to escape things: poverty, war, civil violence, climate change.** Migration is not going on vacation, it is dangerous, difficult and very expensive.

For example, undocumented migrants from Central America to the US literally risk death and dismemberment at the hands of thieves, who, among other things, toss them between train cars. Because the US wants undocumented immigration stopped, Mexico has been coerced into some of the most draconian laws on migrants.

Yet, the draw of being able to make a living and escape violence drives many to attempt the journey. Family members of migrants often assemble cash for the trip, with the expectation that, if the venture is successful, US dollars will trickle back home.

Global Issues says: *"Illegal immigration is a 21st century crisis that will only worsen with the consequences of climate change. In addition to poverty, civil conflict and violence, the increasing high temperatures, widespread droughts, frequent flooding and rising sea levels are leaving parts of the world unlivable. The result will be climate-fueled instability with millions of people likely migrating for their survival.[18]"*

So, an increase in migration is an indicator of social unrest.

Research is complicated by the fact that it takes time to gather and organize data on migration, since much of it is clandestine. As a result, our data is 3 years old. Further, that puts us into the timeline of Covid 19, when much travel was curtailed.

Even so, migration more than doubled between 1990 and 2020; consider this, from the UN IOM World Migration report, 2022:

"Overall, the estimated number of international migrants has increased over the past five decades. The total estimated 281 million people living in a country other than their countries of birth in 2020 was 128 million more than in 1990 and over three times the estimated number in 1970[19]."

We should expect migration to increase, as people flee hunger, poverty, violence and climate change.

How much migration is too much for the system? It can tax individual nations, put more feet under the table for governments; however, most developing nations have a reduced birth rate, so migrants are necessary to fill slots in the population.

We can see that, from a systemic viewpoint, human energy is rebalancing, as many times migrants become higher value producers/consumers to the system. It is bringing young humans into societies which are aging.

On the other hand, **there is no social force more dangerous than a mass of young people with nothing to lose.**

So, migration itself is not really a marker, but it is an indicator of trouble with the system. Immigration might increase the energy in your neighborhood. **In the larger scheme, rather than fearing people with new customs, learn about them, and associate with people with as much to lose as you have, who demonstrate values which you find to be bedrock**, regardless anything else about them, not who they love, not their language, not their dress.

But, keep an eye on migration if you want to try to predict system change for yourself, and find out, if you still have an internet, who is traveling where, and why. (Do try this at home!)

5. What About War?

At this writing, **there are 34 conflicts, "wars" on the planet**. Some are significant, like the US/NATO-Ukrainian conflict with Russia, where many thousands have been killed, and which might lead to nuclear war, and some are minor, where only a hundred or so people are killed each year. Any of them could flare to something bigger, or die out, or most likely, just continue to fester.

However, war is endemic to humans. Clans within tribes had revenge wars; tribes warred over resources, including women; cities warred against tribes for control of resources, and for slaves; nations war for the right to energy, either gold or fossil fuels, or farmland, or trade routes.

Two of the current wars might go nuclear. India and Pakistan fight over Kashmir; US/NATO in Ukraine. In the first instance, there would likely be few bombs, but weather would still be effected, and some have suggested a small nuclear war might slow climate change (because, yes, we are that desperate to find a way to continue burning carbon without dying).

Is there an increase, or a decrease, in the number of wars? Isn't that where we begin, a time series?

However, there are problems with a time series in a matter like this, because wars tend to happen with the kind of frequency that earthquakes do. This means, they are not predictable, and are difficult to define in terms of time and amplitude.

Even so, we have had two world wars (by some definitions) in about a hundred years[20], the potential for a war between NATO and Russia and friends seems high.

War often does not lead to collapse, though it rapidly rearranges a society. Social systems theorists see war as a way for the system to efficiently release stress and move humans and resources around.

It can contribute to local collapse, by siphoning off humans and resources at too rapid a rate, but in general, war is good for business.

Since most wars are for resources (land, environmental products, minerals and oil, and slaves) and geopolitical status, we can expect, as energy and resources, and food, become scarce, there will be more violence and so, more war.

However, a "mutually assured destruction" war, which the Biden administration has commented that we could win, would finish off food and farming for an unknown number of years, and central government, and some key cities, would be destroyed.

Now I Am Going To Quantify My Estimations In Each Of Those Areas

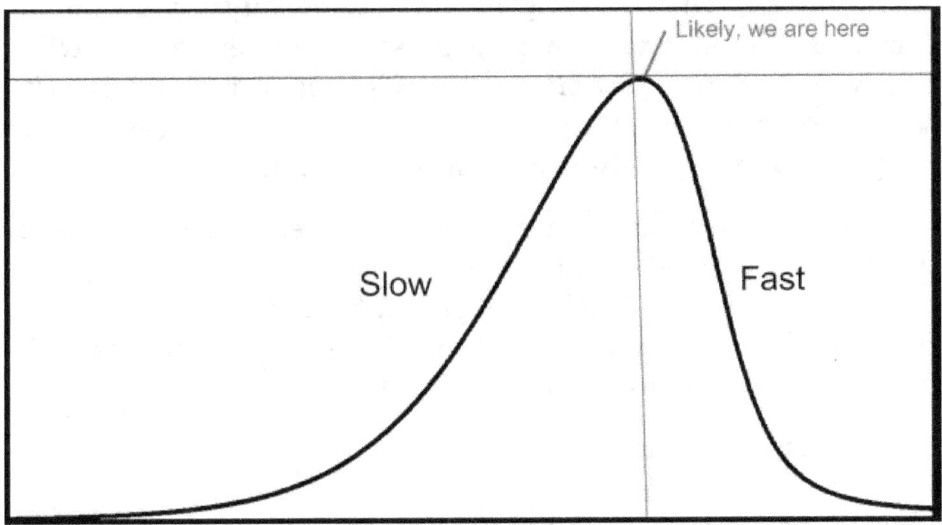

The curve of collapse, with growth being slow, and decline being rapid.

As is so often the case, **I have to just make an educated guess about the actual value of each variable**. Further, the relationship between variables is such that, if for example, oil declines rapidly, social unrest will certainly increase, which will disturb the flow of trade, forcing the need for more energy to make up shortfalls.

We can see that it is a declining feedback loop, with the networks collapsing, driving the collapse of the system. **It increases exponentially, and we can't know that exponent, so we can't accurately figure how rapidly it will go**.

Even so, I will start by quantifying qualities of collapse, and give my estimate of our current status for that variable.

Climate, with 1 being climate before 1750, 5 approaching collapse, and 10 being "Venus type climate": 6.2

Physical energy, debt energy, economy, with 1 being a rapidly growing economy, 5 being a modestly growing economy, and 10 being a destroyed economy with no hope of recovery: 6

Social unrest, with 1 being no unrest, no migration, and no war, and 5 being background protesting, moderate migration, few wars, and 10 a troubled world with major migration, with serious protests and frequent wars, a world in upheaval, with people fleeing everywhere and violence common: 7.5

If we sum those values, and take an average, we get 1 being far from collapse, 5 being stable, and 10 being a shattered global society, and, that makes logical sense, because if they are all 5, then everything should be fine, and if they are 6.5, that is still a long way from collapse.

But collapse is not like that.

If we think about that, we have to wonder, **at what number does collapse happen?**

Here is how it might fall out, with a red line were I think 6.5 would be.

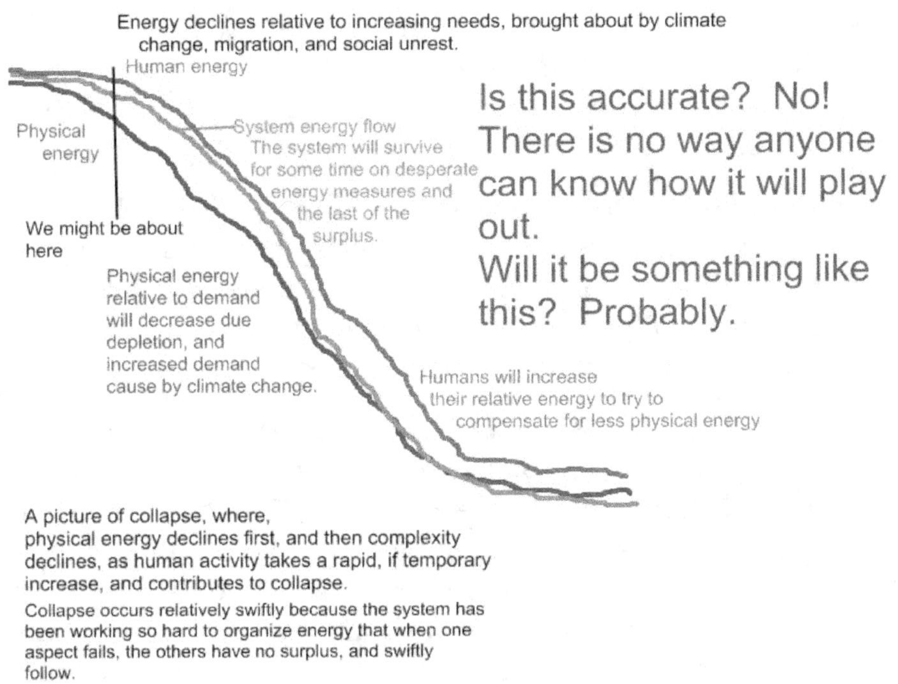

A picture of collapse, where, physical energy declines first, and then complexity declines, as human activity takes a rapid, if temporary increase, and contributes to collapse.

Collapse occurs relatively swiftly because the system has been working so hard to organize energy that when one aspect fails, the others have no surplus, and swiftly follow.

Where will collapse hit first?

We can't know. It might seem that the weakest states would be most susceptible to collapse, but let's think about it.

In some countries, poverty is common, people are hungry often and clean water is scarce. The central system in those countries is already exhibiting the signs of collapse. But many of them pay off huge debts to large banks and corporations, which saps the resources they might otherwise have used to make life better.

If there is a major collapse in hegemonic core nations, where those large economic institutions are, life might actually get better in those places. Vaccines and clinics will disappear, and population will drop, but the cliff is not so steep for them to start with, and they have resilience, not by benefit of having surplus, but because they know how to deal with shortage.

I have decided to map my wild guess to show the order in which

I think collapse will come. Keep in mind, there will be repeated attempts to "reorganize" or "recentralize," some wealthy places may reorganize, assert authority, and begin collecting taxes (see "pay for protection").

In the past, unless the collapse was caused by significant climactic change (for example, some early social systems collapsed because the warming climate melted all the glaciers and the rivers dried up), entities eventually experienced some kind of reorganization, even if only as part of a larger centralized entity.

So, for example, the US should collapse several times over the next 75 years, as regions take over for a unified federal government. However, it is unlikely they will run smoothly, and fighting for status inside the regions might be a problem, and certainly fighting between regions over places that have some value and fall into a discussion where both sides have some claim (let's consider India and Pakistan over Kashmir today).

Things influencing how collapse hits an area are all distance, and resources. Pilfering, taking what can be taken, both from natural resources and from abandoned resources, might persist for a long time, but distance will be the problem.

However, I state up front **there is no way I could know, I could be off by a century, don't do anything based on the outcome of this example**!

Nonetheless, it is the best estimate I can make. I encourage you to do your own estimates, based on your data and rationales.

Predicting the timing and order of collapse accurately would be worth a great deal, and no doubt, people with money to spend are working on the problem, and, they will have much more data and much more up to date data, but their likelihood of success is really only a little better than ours.

That is the reality we deal with, but it shouldn't overwhelm us. **Being able to see a foot in front of your feet is better** than walking in utter darkness. It is work to predict, and takes courage to do it though you know the strength of your predictions is modest. We just work on our skills.

Not Every Minute Will Be Bad

The things that are of lasting importance will still be important. Opportunities appear for local people to provide products now provided by global corporations. During collapse, people make money.

Currently, in many places, a backyard rabbit grower can't sell a butchered rabbit. Many do, because there is often a brisk market, but it is illegal because the growing area, butchering area and meat have not been inspected, there is no liability insurance or bookkeeping and so on. The cost of just setting up such a business would take more rabbits than a backyard grower can grow. **If there are no government cops, rabbits will become worth a great deal, and no one will object to their sale.**

Likewise, if we aren't killed by climate change, as McPherson believes, or by nuclear war, as many believe, life will continue and even get better. A shrinking population means diminishing resources have to go less far. The value of each person increases.

Which logically brings us to a review!

7. EVERY FAMILY'S REVIEW

Family is important.   Your family are those people who share your fate, who work with you to live.

Calm is a super power.

People are the medium through which energy in the system passes.   This is because we have propensities which cause most of us to do things like most of us do. We need affiliation, a social index to which we can evaluate and try to increase or maintain our status, people in our network.

People do what they do because they have emotions, most of which refer to a person's status, and their reliability and that of others they interact with.   We know people interact with each other most often within a social sphere of similarity, familiarity and proximity. Understanding these things about humans makes their behavior relatively simple, but still unpredictable in the long term.

We live in a world of complex systems. It is very difficult to predict complex systems accurately, but we can make short term guesses or "predictions" with some accuracy, and learn to make longer term predictions which offer us an opportunity to make informed decisions.

The complex system we live in isn't just a jumble, it has form, and we can imagine, or even see, this form as networks. We just watch the networks, see the flow of energy, of people, goods, and debt, and determine the energy return on the energy investment for our family.

We can have a methodology, that is a logical way to make sense of what we see, and apply that methodology to many issues. However, we always understand that when we predict, it is an informed guess, and not a certainty. Even so, **an informed guess is likely better than a blind guess**.

Methodology is energy intensive; the family must ceaselessly gather and report information from the world, and someone has to organize it, and people have to make tough decisions about the values of things. **The family has to be dispassionate regarding the methodology, and in particular, how they gauge and quantify resources.**

We realize and accommodate the advantages and weaknesses of tracking variables over time, the time series, kept on several key variables. Those variables represent energy moving in networks. The more data we have on them, and the more we know about the networks on which they rely, the better our understanding and predictions can be.

Making sense of the complex system does not solve all dilemmas. The family needs to do research, draw conclusions about the energy return on energy investment of each decision, not just for that moment, but for a future where bad news is common.

We might have to live through hard times; we are alive because thousands of ancestors lived through hard times and beat the odds.

Now, we try.

Go out and justify the survival of your ancestors!

[1]You have a short, pleasantly suburban walk of twenty minutes to work; a little longer in winter. You plan your morning by it, and mesh it with important tasks like helping children and touching base with family, organizing laundry and making a healthy lunch. The route that gives you this efficiency includes a street which parallels a main artery, which you avoid, because of noise and delays crossing streets. However, down the block, a new family moves in. They have a large, snapping and snarling dog tied to a long chain. Since the dog is restricted to their property, it is not a public nuisance, but you are afraid of dogs and it jangles your nerves. (The dog throws himself at the end of the chain; how securely is it fastened?) You can simply cross the street, but that puts you moving against the other people hurrying to work, and puts you on the wrong side of the street to turn to work, causing you to cross the street twice. You decide to walk to the busy street, though the new route takes four minutes longer, adding a fifth to the time you need, which rushes other well timed morning duties. Unconvincing? Not a dog, a crack house.

[2]The Holocene is described as beginning about 12,000 years ago when the last glacial maximum began to recede.

[3]E. O. Wilson, biologist and multiple disciplinary scholar, for example, has stated that humans are eusocial.

[4]NASA image of Houston Texas at night, 2010, https://earthobservatory.nasa.gov/images/43196/houston-texas-at-night

[5]NASA image of Tokyo Japan at night, 2008, https://earthobservatory.nasa.gov/images/8683/tokyo-at-night

[6]Census data on manufacturing revenue, 2023, https://www.census.gov/econ/currentdata/

[7]The idea of 1.5C is that the total global temperature increases by 1.5 degrees Celsius above the temperature in the mid 1800s. It is feared by most climatologists that it will reach 2C, by which point all bets are off.

[8]https://www.ipcc.ch/reports/

[9]   Limits to Growth, By Donella Meadows et al, 1972. Subtitled "A Report for the Club of Rome's Project on the Predicament of Mankind." https://www.library.dartmouth.edu/digital/digital-collections/limits-growth

[10]   Near-Term Resilience, Persistent Challenges   July 2023 https://www.imf.org/en/Publications/WEO/Issues/2023/07/10/world-economic-

outlook-update-july-2023

[11] https://www.worldbank.org/en/publication/global-economic-prospects

[12] Statista Global Energy Prices; Statista Reseach Department https://www.statista.com/topics/1323/energy-prices/

[13] IMF Fossil Fuel Subsidies Data: 2023 Update Simon Black ; Antung A. Liu ; Ian W.H. Parry ; Nate Vernon August 2023 https://www.imf.org/en/Publications/WP/Issues/2023/08/22/IMF-Fossil-Fuel-Subsidies-Data-2023-Update-537281#

[14] If it is still possible, read the article here: https://ourfiniteworld.com/2023/08/31/fossil-fuel-imports-are-already-constrained/

[15] https://globalnews.ca/news/6087849/protests-around-the-world-reasons/

[16] https://www.csis.org/analysis/age-mass-protests-understanding-escalating-global-trend

[17] An Analysis of World Protests 2006–2020 Isabel Ortiz, Sara Burke, Mohamed Berrada & Hernán Saenz Cortés

First Online: 04 November 2021 https://link.springer.com/chapter/10.1007/978-3-030-88513-7_2

[18] https://www.globalissues.org/news/2021/10/27/29174 Illegal Immigration: A 21st Century Crisis

[19] https://worldmigrationreport.iom.int/wmr-2022-interactive/

[20] There is a good case to be made for the proposition that WWI and WWII were the same war, that the Treaty of Versailles and subsequent treaties weakened Germany's economy and set up the social unrest that elected Adolf Hitler.